A SNAPSHOT IN TIME

Fruit Tramps and Vagrants

R.S. Poynter

Bizy Enterprises, Inc. -Publisher-Mesa, Arizona.

A SNAPSHOT IN TIME
FRUIT TRAMPS AND VAGRANTS

Author: R.S. Poynter

Published by:
Bizy Enterprises, Inc.
13 Leisure World
Mesa, Az. 85206

Photos used with the permission of the US Library of Congress, The Dorothea Lange Collection.

Copyright 2013
ISBN: 978-0-972-2621-3-2, first printed edition
Publishing date: 7/15/13

TABLE OF CONTENTS

Dedicated To:

Betty (girl) Jean Taylor

I am proud and honored to
help you tell this story

A special thanks goes out to Shiloh Penland & Sherry Emery.

Thank you to the editors for their involvement.

Thank you to Erin Sheriff Design, for creating a beautiful cover and an interior layout design.

Erin Sheriff Design

Acknowledgements

I want to thank my family for allowing me the time and resources to accomplish this book.

Thank you especially to my wife (Brenda) for her support when things were difficult. She was always encouraging, and she would say; "this is too important of a story to leave behind".

Thank you to all who so graciously have given me feedback, as I asked so many questions in search of the truth of that time from those who lived it.

Thank you Betty "Girl","MOM", for allowing me to tell your story, I know it was difficult at times as you had to remember times past, and what it still means in your life today.

You have persevered throughout your life. You stand tall and proud, as much today as you always have. You are a champion to your family, and I hope this will help to fulfill your dreams of telling others about your life as a "Fruit Tramp".

Introduction

Eighty years ago a girl was born into a world that would reject her even as a small girl. Living and working on the fringes of the communities where they scraped out a living and then were told to get on down the road before they were arrested for being vagrants.

This story is a Snapshot In Time and the real life story of that little girl, "Betty Girl". Shortly after the Great Depression and just prior to World War Two the role of women and children could be classified as, subservient to men for there own good because it was believed that women and children could not exist without men to provide for them.

World War Two set the United States and the old belief's of society into a drastic period of change, the beginning of the women's revolution and changing roles in society.

Betty Girl had no idea at the time what cost would have to be paid or how long the price would have to be paid for the change to equality and fairness in the work place. The fight continues and the price has been very high for many of those who demand change and are willing to give their all for it, the cost of that fight for Betty Girl is still being paid today as she is eighty years of age.

This story, the life of Betty Girl will bring you to that time and then take you through the daily struggle of society in a "mans world".

CHAPTER ONE

BETTY "GIRL"

"Free of charge, Ma'am," those were the words Momma heard from the doctor at the hospital where I was born on the morning of December 10, 1934.

Momma was asking the doctor what it was going to cost for having a baby in a hospital, as I was the first of her three children not 'home delivered.'

Momma must have been relieved to hear those words, and I must have been in the room when she was told that, because I spent a good deal of my childhood feeling like I owed everybody something.

See, nothing is free, not completely free, everything has a cost. If you don't pay for it now you certainly will later - this was no different.

I paid for it with my childhood, wondering why I felt the way I did and never really getting an answer.

I was the third daughter of Homer,(Daddy) and Myrtle's(Momma),growing family. There would be four more girls and one boy. Midge was born in 1930, Donnie in 1932 and me in 1934. The next three were four years apart with Curtis in 1937, Doris in 1940 and Alma in 1943. The baby was Andie and she was born just one year after Alma in 1944, Alma would be the last.

As I said, I was the first to be born in a hospital .The hospital was named, Morningside Catholic Hospital of Tulsa.

At the time, Morningside was not only the largest hospital in the state; it was the tallest building, too. Daddy later told me the government was the one who put up the money for its construction to help create jobs called the, "President's New Deal," New construction also would attract more business to the area that had been suffering so badly for so long; in part because of the Great Depression and the devastation from the Dust Bowl ten years prior.

However, that was only part of the reason poor people got free medical care, it also would help pay off the government money loan requirements. Momma said Daddy never stopped complaining about the government and banks. He said they were, "inkah'hoots to take people's money".

I guess Daddy always was complaining about the government, and Momma acted like she never got tired of listening. She said she would just sit and listen as Daddy would tell her how things should be, and the whole time she was thinking about sitting somewhere quiet in a grove of shade trees with her feet stuck down in the cool grass.

As I got older it still was the same way. I remember hearing Daddy going on about things, and I thought my Daddy was the smartest man in the world with him knowing so much about everything. The older I got; the smarter he got. Some things never change.

We had so little, all our worldly possessions fit into the back of whatever old, broken-down car we were living out of at the time. The country continued in deep economic depression, and jobs were as scarce as honest politicians.

Opportunities for destitute families only came if we were willing to stay on the hunt and sacrifice whatever was necessary to take advantage of something that would certainly cost us more than it was worth. The depression made people do things they otherwise would not have done. People really did care about each other, but when there is only one loaf of bread and your kids are hungry, how you think about charity to others changes.

Daddy didn't have a car when I was born, and there was no such thing as an ambulance to pick up folks. I was told he talked the ranch foreman into taking Momma to the hospital when she told him it was, "time."

Every big ranch had a foreman who looked after the cabins and hired hands. He made sure the work was done and watched after who was working well, who was lazy and who was just looking for a place to stay.

There was no room in the foremen's small truck, so Daddy had to hitch a ride after he got someone to take care of the other two girls, Donnie and Midge. He got to the hospital early the next morning, before I was born. He told me later that the foreman let him take the day off to get us back home from the hospital.

Some of the parents in the camp would watch other families' kids if it was an emergency or something like having a baby - all you had to do was ask.

Daddy left my two older sisters with a black family they had known from years of traveling and staying in the same camps. He had to leave Donnie and Midge there even though Midge would always cry when that family took care of her. Midge cried about everything it seemed, and leaving her there was no different. Momma said she thought it was because they had two young boys who were about five. They were loud and always wrestling around. Momma thought it was because of Midge having polio and getting hit on her legs.

Midge later told me it was because they were black, and she was afraid of the difference in how they looked.

As I got older I played with those two boys and many others like them. We all were just kids, working in the fields and living the same way - none of us thought we were any different no matter what color we were.

2

I asked Momma what she remembered about the day I was born, and the first thing she talked about was the weather, "It was cold and there was snow on the ground." Daddy just said, "It was forty one degrees and cloudy, snow on the ground, as I remember it."

Weather was a big deal in those days because migrants like us were living in cabins with only a small wood stove for heat. People were freezing to death. In the winter we were freezing. In the summer we were sweating like pigs.

As I was born in December and Momma was hoping the winter wouldn't be too bad because it was harder taking care of a baby in the winter cold. "A lot of kids got sick with phenomena and died 'cause of not having a doctor, and poor nutrition."

Momma later told me she delivered me in a Hospital because Donnie, my older sister, was more than 13 pounds when she was born. The midwife told Momma, "You might want to go to the hospital this time Myrtle, that last one almost killed you. If you are gonna keep havin' kids that are half grown, you better be with a doctor."

Momma used a midwife, and had the first two girls at home, as did many in those days, hospitals were for the wealthy. Momma was told that because we were so poor, the government was helping out people having kids, and we didn't have to pay for the hospital or the doctor.

Momma later told me she didn't really like having kids at the hospital because they acted like she was trash. They wouldn't even give her a pillow to prop up her head. Momma said, "I think they put me in the same bed as the lady who was leavin' out when we showed up to the hospital. When I got in the bed it was still warm and the covers were all wrinkled."

"I didn't complain 'cause I was afraid you would be as big as Donnie, so I did whatever they told me. I didn't know any better and was just learning about hospitals and how they did things. I had never even been to a hospital before; I was just a kid and was scared".

Momma said she was relieved when I was born and only weighed 11 pounds. I was blonde haired, green eyed, and I had Okie-white skin. Momma said I looked more like Daddy than her. Daddy was awful proud of that fact and made sure he asked everybody that would listen if I looked like him.

After I was born, the nurse put me in a paper box in the maternity ward, not like the rich kids who were wrapped up nice in a metal bed with pretty blankets and their full name on the end of the bed for all their family to see.

My paper box had my first name and gender, that's all. When he looked through the window for me he said the end of my box said, 'Betty, Girl,' nothing more.

Daddy called me Betty Girl the rest of my life. I don't remember him ever calling me anything but that. Funny how those things stick with you! As I was growing up other kids would ask me why Daddy called me that.

I'd tell them, "cause he does, that's all!'

I guess I always felt special, different than the other kids because I was the only one Daddy ever did that with. Sometimes, all I had to hang onto was the little things.

Well, I don't know if it mattered if you were born at home or at a hospital but it was better for Mamma because all the rest of the kids were big -11 and 12 pounds. After me, she had the rest of the kids in a hospital, just to be safe.

We were poor and the government was paying for it, so Momma took advantage of what they were offering. She said it was nice because the hospital was warm and she didn't have to smell the smoke from the wood stove while she was giving birth.

Momma used to joke when I was little about having kids. When we would see someone who was pregnant she would say, "havin' kids is like passin' a watermelon." We were young and didn't really understand at the time what that meant, but we laughed because we knew watermelons were big.

I learned later on when I began having my own kids what that meant; and yes, I had one '13 pound watermelon, the last one!

I contracted Typhoid Fever shortly after I was born and had to stay in the hospital for several weeks. I was in isolation, and the hospital tried to keep everybody out of my room. Momma said my Uncle Lyle, Daddy's brother, showed up and told them he had already had it, and wanted to come in and see me, of course they told him, "no".

Well, there was some big commotion down the hall. Momma later told me it was aunt Lilly, Uncle Lyle's wife. Everybody went to go see what was going on, and that's when Uncle Lyle slipped into my room to see me.

Momma and Daddy was afraid to come in and see me because they were afraid the other kids would get the fever too, since we all lived in that small one-room cabin. Uncle Lyle did it because he would not have to be around Donnie or Midge and take a chance of giving it to them

I guess uncle Lyle ripped into those nurses when he found me all bruised up and crying. He accused them of beating me, and convinced them that he would beat them if he found another mark on me. I just remember being scared and alone.

Momma said they treated me real good after that. I guess it was pretty common for kids to be treated that way back then, especially when one cried all the time because they were hurting, sick, and alone.

Medicine was not cheap and if you didn't have the money to pay for it, you just weren't getting any. Nobody was going to make the hospital give it away. I think it's still like that today. Some things never change.

Momma told me that when they released me from the hospital, we got a ride back to the cabin from the garbage man that Daddy knew. They had lived next door for a while and Daddy had made friends with him.

George also hailed from Missouri where Daddy was born, and I guess that was enough. They both were about the same age, and Daddy would tell stories about him and George "eatin the same dirt" on this and that farm all over Missouri.

I thank God for George - he was a good friend to our family, someone that could be trusted. My folks said he was a Godsend, which meant they liked him.

We lived in a one room cabin at a place outside Tulsa called, Medco Hill. It was on the road next to the Tulsa City Dump. Daddy said it was a good cabin for those days because it had a wood stove and tar paper on the out-side to keep the wind out. There was one light hanging from the rafters and a water pump, just outside the front door. It had one window with newspaper curtains and a sink that drained out onto the ground and into the culvert ditch for the field.

The outhouse was just out back on the edge of the orchard, and Daddy would tell stories about how it was the best darn outhouse he ever saw - he said it didn't even smell.

I guess it was because the dump was so smelly, you couldn't smell the outhouse.

He would laugh about that outhouse until he cried. He and Mamma knew something they weren't telling. I would see them look at each other and then look away again. We would ask what was so funny, but they never told us.

They were living at the Medco Hill dump when Momma got pregnant with me, I always wondered?

Daddy said it was good livin' there by the city dump because the garbage man would drop off good stuff. Mostly stuff we could sell in town. Sometimes old bread and stuff from the bakery, too.

The grocery store would throw out old fruits and vegetables, and it was

being picked up by other families who were hungry and poor like us. The guy at the store liked Daddy, so he would put some back for us and we would pick it up at the end of the day or first thing the next morning. Daddy said it was mostly potatoes and carrots, that's all there was, and he was grateful for it.

A dime or two and you had enough for some meat to go with the potatoes. Momma said they could buy bones from the Butcher and he would give them the ones with a little meat left on 'em. She said it sure made a good pot of beans.

We ate beans every day, so it was good to have some with meat. As I look back, we must have looked like a bunch of wild dogs when we would take those bones out of the pot and start scraping our teeth against 'em for a small piece of meat. Funny, I can still hear all that smackin,' - like we were eatin' steak.

My folks went to the dump at the end of the day to check and see if they could find anything we could eat or sell, for money to buy food. Momma would have Midge watch me while she helped Daddy look around.

Daddy said he had a few fights over stuff up there and was afraid he was going to get killed over something stupid. I know he had a temper and he would take it to someone pretty quick. Everybody was hungry and would fight for their family to have something to eat.

Momma told me that Daddy got into some pretty bad fights when people would get into the stuff George left hidden for us at the dump. There was a small shed on the edge of the dump by our cabin and George would hide things there if Daddy was not around. People started watching and after George left, they would go take it.

The same people came up to the dump every day just like us. When Daddy found out who it was, he would call 'em out. He tried run everyone else out of the dump and acted like he owned the place to keep it for himself - it usually worked. People were afraid of him.

It was the depression and with no jobs to be had, Daddy and the older girls would pick up glass alongside the roads and behind some of the stores and restaurants in town. Every once in a while he said the people would run him off from behind the store saying they were stealing, but he didn't care, his family was hungry. I was too young to remember those times, but when I got older, we were still picking up glass along the roadside. Some things never change.

Tulsa was as good a place as any to be in the early thirties. Daddy said him and Momma knew that part of the country, and it always was kind of Daddy's home. Momma and Daddy had other kin in that part of the country and it was best to keep some family close by in case we needed extra help. None of them had any money, but it was a family, and that means a lot for people who have so little.

The government was helping folks around there, and giving a little food and medicine to impoverished families. Several local churches were there to help as well. At times, Momma would tell Daddy she wanted to stay and set up for good; that never flew with him and off we would go to the next town.

Because my sister Midge had Polio, she needed to be seen to by a doctor every so often. Daddy liked the doc they had in Tulsa, because he was smart and he took good care of my sister Midge. Daddy also said that doctor treated her "like a real person" and always found a way to get the medicine she needed, so it seemed like we always ended up back there no matter where we were through the harvest season.

Midge was in a lot of pain because of the Polio, and I remember from a young age, her crying and holding her legs asking Momma to make it stop. It was really hard for her.

Polio was pretty common at that time and lots of folks had it. Nobody really knew what caused it, and lots of people said it was because we were dirty. We were poor but Momma never let us be dirty, even if she had to wash us in the ditch water by the fields.

People talked as if us kids were not even standing there, telling Momma to keep her dirty kids back from theirs so they wouldn't get sick. I hated them for that, and I wanted them to get sick like my sister to teach them a

lesson. People were so cruel to us because we were poor and didn't look like them. We couldn't help it that we were poor any more then they had anything to do with their family having money; when you're a kid you just have to accept the hand God lent to ya!

No one deserves to be sick like Midge was, and have people look at her funny like she was some kind of freak. I tried to stick up for her all my life, against the family or anybody else that hurt her. Midge and I were very close. She took care of me when I was very young, and then I took care of her when I got older. I never believed she got sick because we were dirty. All of us kids were the same way and none of the rest of us got Polio.

We were family; no matter what we had or did not have, it did not change blood. Even with all the fightin' we did through the years, we still looked after each other when we were kids.

We all lived the same life with Momma and Daddy but did it our own way; we each had our own personality and beliefs and worked to accept each other.

I learned how to be poor at a very young age. I remember looking at myself in the mirror and wondering what others thought about me. What do they see? Is it different than what I see of myself? Knowing what I know about me - things you will never see - I am more than poor!

CHAPTER TWO

Momma & Daddy

M omma and Daddy met in Missouri sometime in 1929. Daddy's brother was going around with Momma's older sister and that's how they met. Momma and Daddy married, and his brother and Momma's sister got married also.

I know that Daddy and his brother were working for the Missouri Highway Department, and that's how they happen to be in that part of the country. They moved along with the work crew, and lived in tents next to where they were clearing trees out of the way of the new interstate highway that was working its way through the Joplin area.

Daddy said the land was so flat that if you stood on the back of the wagon you could see for a hundred miles in any direction.

The farms were big in that part of the country; they were big corporate operations that were selling to the folks in the East, where there was money.

Daddy said they had been working near a big ranch; it had a farmhouse that stuck up out of the landscape like a castle. It was a big white three story house -taller than the trees around it and had two big barns.

He said, "We were working about four or five miles away from that farm and we was all talking about what that kind of life that must be –livin' in a big house like that. We was talking and dreaming about tomorrow and how it would be if we lived there. Sometimes, we just needed to dream away from the back breaking work we were doing and the constant hundred-degree heat."

Daddy and his brother worked on the crew that blew up the tree stumps the mule teams couldn't pull out, "Some of the tree stumps were so big from those old oak trees that you could hide a team of horses behind 'em, and the hickories were just as big."

Daddy told me that some of those trees had been there for a hundred years or more.

The trees were cut up and sold for firewood in Joplin and some of it was sold to make furniture. He said the firewood was awful good but would break your back loading it for people.

Daddy said they sold and loaded firewood some days when they were waiting for more blasting supplies to earn a little extra money. The blasting foreman sold it to locals who brought their wagons out from town.

Daddy's brother, Joshua, was older and, "was the guy who drove the wagon back and forth to pick up dynamite from the train rail yard in Joplin, and then deliver it out to us."

Daddy said they also worked with an old Irishman everybody called "Barrel." Daddy said he was "big as a barrel." I guess he was okay with the guys calling him that, or he would have put a stop to it. Daddy described him as a big Irishman who wore coveralls all the time because he couldn't find suspenders big enough to fit.

Daddy used to always joke that they had to put a stripe on Barrel so they would know if he was walkin' or rollin!' I was much older before I understood that joke. As kids we always laughed anyway because it sounded funny.

As Daddy told it, he and Barrel were blowing stumps all day and it was hot. He said, "Me and Barrel was tired and just trying to get through the sun-up to sun-down schedule. We put some sticks of dynamite under this big old hickory and got the hell out of there, and waited.

After a bit, me and Barrel started lookin' at each other wonderin' why it never went off. We figured the fuse went out when I stuffed it under that big stump,'cause I had to use a pretty long stick to push it way under."

I don't know why Daddy was the guy who had to go pull it back out to try again, but that's what happened.

Daddy said he no more than shoved that same dam stick under there to try and get the dynamite back out, and it went off.

He said he don't remember much more. The rest of what happened, he said Barrel told him later when he came to see him at that big farmhouse - the one they had worked by just a few days earlier - where he was stayin' trying to heal up from all the damage done by the explosion.

Barrel told him, "When you put that stick under the stump, it let out a crack and dust went to flyin.' I wasn't sure if you was alive or dead. I was alookin' for ya, and yellin' out to ya, and wasn't sure even where to look for

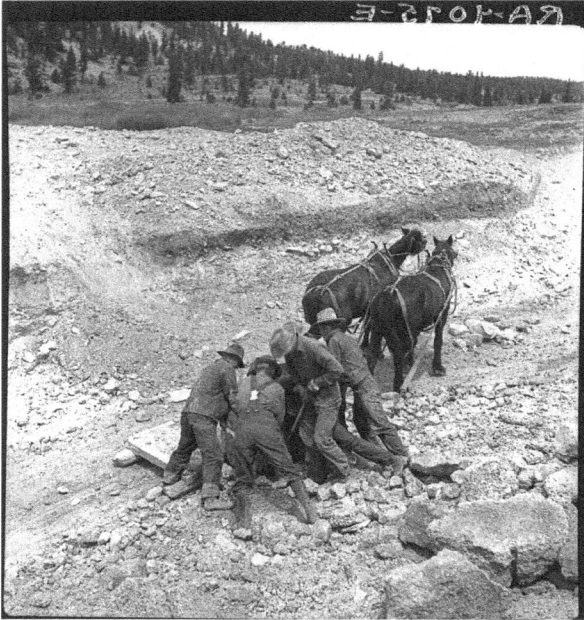

ya. I was afraid I was gonna find ya all blew to pieces and dead. And, since we was the only men out there, that far from the other crew cause of the dynamite, I wasn't even sure if they would know we needed help."

Barrel continued, "We were damned lucky Homer, your brother was a commin' out to get us at the end of the day. He had that old mule all loaded up with supplies for the next day. Joshua helped me look for ya, and he found you in a big ol' hole about fifty feet from where that big old stump was layin.' I didn't even see ya 'cause my eyes were filled with dirt from the blast, and I think I must have walked past you a couple times. You were all covered with dirt and layin' face down.

Well, you were bleedin' badly and your left hand was gone. We were tryin' to figure what to do. Then, Joshua took off his belt and wrapped it around your wrist and just snatched you up over his big broad shoulders so quick it makes my head spin just thinkin' about it.

Well, Joshua, he was scared for ya, and even as big as he is, he ran you over to that old mule - I just stayed outta his way. I already had pulled off the load of supplies. Over you went across that mules back like a sack of taters; boy that was something to see.

Joshua took off like a bolt of lighten to the big old farmhouse just a couple miles back, 'cause we was an hour ride from town and he didn't think you would make it that long with you bleedin' so bad.

"Joshua took off with you on the mule and him a runnin' out front draggin' that poor old mule along. Well that mule didn't stand a chance of stoppin' him and I was runnin' as fast as I could go just to try and keep up.

He was out-runnin' the both of us, lickety-split, and neither man nor beast could slow him down. You were floppin' all over on that mule's back, and the whole time I was a thinkin' you were dead", or would be from the beattin' that ride was given ya.

"I had never seen Joshua move so quickly, and the way the two of you fight all the time, I didn't think he had it in 'em to help you like he did that day. When we got close to the farmhouse he was hollerin' out so loud he could be heard in the next county. He was yellin' over and over, 'Help, my brother's hurt bad.' By the time we got up to the house two old ladies was standin' out front lookin' to see what all the hollerin' was about.

As soon as they saw you, they started yellin' and runnin' and grabbin' things to help. The old lady with no teeth kept tellin' me to do somethin' but I couldn't understand her, and the longer I was standin' there tryin' to catch my breath, the louder she was yellin.'

Those two ladies got you up on an old table and started pullin' off your shirt, tearin' at it, and bitin' at it like a couple wild dogs. Damnedest thing you ever saw, Homer. I was so out of breath and scared for you I couldn't even laugh, but I wanted to."

"Anyway, they got some water and a bunch of rags and started wiping' and washin' like you was a new born baby. Old Joshua was tryin' to help and they was shovin' him back and yellin' for him to stay out of the way.

Well, he was tired and couldn't put up a fight, so we just stood back and did what we was told."

"They worked on you, for what must ah been an hour before they even looked up.

I couldn't believe my eyes when they stuck your arm in a pot o' boilin' water. You was squirmin' all over but not makin' a sound. They held it in there and then would pull it out, and have a look at it real close, then back in again. I thought they was plum crazy what they was doin' but the bleedin' finally stopped and they was sayin', 'we can save him, we can save him.' "

"There wasn't much of your hand left after the blast, and they was workin' to get the rest of it off there.

They was puttin' Bag Balm on it from the barn and twistin' the skin around kind of funny, like wringin' out an old rag.

I smelt your skin burnin' and wondered how you could live through what was going on. They was dumpin' whisky on the end of your arm, then puttin' it back in that damned boilin' pot."

"Well, that seemed to go on forever, and then all of a sudden, they had you wrapped up in some of them rags they had been boilin' in the same old pot as your arm. That's it, it was over."

"That was it, and they told us to go and check back in a few days to see how you was doin.'

But, Joshua was not leavin. 'He told me to go on back and let the shift boss know what happened. That old mule was rested up, so off I went back to the main camp to tell everybody what happened."

"Joshua showed up a couple days later and told us you were alive and doin' good. He said he knew we are all sad about what happened, and hoped you would be okay. We knew you would have a hard life because of it."

Daddy said when old Barrel looked down at his missing hand he about cried, and told him how sorry he was for what had happened.

Daddy said he never saw Barrel after that last visit at the farmhouse.

Daddy said he knew the other men would have to keep working, and could not wait for him to heal up and rejoin them. He knew he would never see any of them again, because the railroad would not let him work for them again with a missing hand. He was right.

Daddy and Joshua both ended their job with the State that day and never worked for the government again.

Joshua stayed with him at the ranch and worked around the barns repairing farm equipment - he was good working on stuff like that.

Daddy said the two old ladies watched over him like he was their own. He said him and Joshua stayed there for several weeks, until he was strong enough to move on to Oklahoma.

Daddy and Joshua never did see any other men working around the place but figured some men were there because he could hear the teams of horses being hitched up early every morning.

Daddy said a man, who claimed to be a doctor, came out to see him once - a couple days after the accident -and was more trouble than he was worth. He said, "He didn't do nothin' but poke on it and ask some questions about what happened."

"It was the damnedest thing, that doctor asking what happened. If he was a doctor he would be able to see, 'I got my hand blowed off!' "

Daddy was tough and had to be in those days because nobody was going to take care of you for nothing. Everybody had to work because there was nobody to just hand out money and food like there is today.

Daddy had a big hand, and when you shook his hand, you knew a man was on the other end of that hand. He could hurt ya without even trying, he was so strong. It was always fun to watch him take hold of another man's hand and then you could see them look down at their hand to see if they still had it after Daddy let go.

Sometimes, we could hear their joints poppin' when Daddy was squeezing it, and he would do it just to see the look on their faces.

He kept his left stump in his pants pocket when he would meet people, especially the ranch foreman when we were looking for work. Most of the time they never knew he had only one hand. He could pick as much with that one hand as most anybody else could with two good hands.

His hand had been gone for several years before he met Mamma, and he had found a way to manage very well with just the one hand.

Momma was 17 when she married Daddy. She said she was looking for a good man - tough, handsome and strong. And, although Daddy had only one hand, she said he was as tough and strong as they came.

Daddy was 34 and was looking for a young wife. Momma was young and tough and looking for an older man, you had to be tough in those days.

The drought, the depression, the Dust Bowl, I don't know how much people can take. I don't know how they made it. It took great strength and courage to make it through, and many did not.

Momma used to talk about the end of some families. It wasn't until much later in life that I began to understand what she meant. She was talking about families in which everyone dies. None of them left to carry on, and the family name ended for all time.

Momma talked about how proud she was that they survived, and could carry the family names on thru the future. Her family lived and worked as sharecroppers scattered throughout Arkansas, and they had been as far back as she could remember.

Daddy, too, had been farming with his family as sharecroppers for as many generations as he could remember. Farming was what they knew and were good at - and after Daddy's accident, it's all he could get work doing.

He would get work at some of the factories for a short time, but as soon as they found out about his missing hand, they would send him away.

They didn't have laws back then that protected people with handicaps. People were just afraid of his missing hand, as if it were a disease, and would not let him stay even though he could do the work, and would have even worked for less money.

There was nothing Daddy couldn't do like any other man, and in fact, he could roll a cigarette better and faster than most. Daddy smoked all his life, until he died at the age of 98.

I often wondered how he made it with just the one hand. I thought about what it meant to him as a man. Did he feel less than other men with two hands? I asked myself if I ever saw him back down from anything in his life; and the answer was "no." I guess when I think about it, it makes sense that he was no different than anybody else.

He only had one heart, and he loved like everybody else He only had one mind, and he thought like everybody else. He only had one soul, and he believed in God like everybody else. He only had one hand, and he provided for his family, like everybody else.

So, was he different than anybody else?

I guess each of us have to decide that for ourselves.

CHAPTER THREE

All Nine Of Us Now

There were nine of us now, me, five sisters, one brother, Momma and Daddy. Midge was the oldest, then Donnie, me: Betty, my only brother: Curtis, then Doris, Alma and Bella, the baby.

Although Midge was the oldest, she was never made to work or do much of anything because of her polio. Sometimes, she used it as an excuse so she wouldn't have to do anything, especially on the really cold days when none of us wanted to go outside for any reason.

My older sister Donnie was a quiet child, as I remember, but as she got older she got to be a real smart mouth with everybody. I suppose that was her way to keep everyone at bay so they wouldn't question her about what she was or was not doing. Momma said it was her defense mechanism - since Donnie did not want to do anything she was told to do by Momma, or her teachers, she would keep them away by being mean and nasty.

Me, I minded my manners and wanted to be smart and go to school. I was willing to work hard in the fields for the family and do whatever I had to so I could help all of us out. As it was, I was taken advantage of most of my childhood because of my willingness to help.

Curtis was a spoiled brat, being the only boy, so Daddy looked after him most of the time. You better watch yourself around Curtis because Daddy would scold us or give a good beating if we bothered Curtis. As Curtis got older, he learned how to use that, and acted like he was our boss. He was like that all his life - bossy.

Doris, we called her Doty, was a mean kid. She was never happy and always mad about something. If she did not have something to be mad about, then she would make something up. I think she used that to keep people away and it worked. She was bitter about everything and acted like we were all trying to get her. Nobody ever made her as mad as she made herself though. It was kind of funny.

Alma was a free spirit, and did not seem to care about anything - it was like she knew something we didn't. I always wondered why she seemed to be so free-spirited, even when it was bad for us. No food, no water, broken down on the side of another hot or frozen highway, and she was singing or humming like nothing mattered except what was in her mind. Daddy would tell Momma that Alma was crazy like her. Momma would tell Daddy that she needed to be crazy to live with him. I guess both of them were right.

Amanda (Bella) was the baby. She managed to play that role very well, and used it to her advantage. However, she had to, so she would not get walked all over by the rest of us. Bella was the fattest kid because she got most of the food, being the baby and all. I liked to take care of Bella. She and I were pretty close as we got older. The older girls started to separate themselves from the rest of the family. But, Bella and I stayed close most of our lives.

My grandmother traveled with us and lived with us for many years after grandpa died. She had nowhere else to go. We just called her, 'Little Granny. 'Little Granny was a McIntosh and Scottish by blood. Momma said there were none tougher than McIntosh. I wondered for a long time what that meant, until I realized it was because her maiden name was McIntosh.

Little Granny was good to us kids. She would hide extra food in her apron pocket when we got something from the church or the farm foremen, to share with us kids later.

Little Granny was so small, the pocket on the front of the apron, ended up on the side when she tied it tight against her waist. That little side pocket was a place where we found small pieces of extra bread and candy, Andie (Bella) was the baby so she got the little treasures Granny kept there most of the time .

I think she kept stuff there for when Midge was crying about her legs hurting. Granny would give it to her when

she would cradle her and try to help settle her down. I would see Midge reach in there; Little Granny would try to hide it so she could keep it from the rest of us kids. I didn't care about that too much because Little Granny

16

sometimes would let us have it, too.

Little Granny was awful good to me and Midge - she helped us carry our lug boxes in the field, and helped us drag our cotton sacks when they were full. She always worked next to me and Midge, because Midge was not able to do much work with her bad legs. Daddy would get mad, thinking Midge was lazy and not working as hard as the rest of us, so Little Granny helped take up the slack. Daddy did not yell at Little Granny, and she wouldn't let him yell at us, either.

Little Granny had to watch out for all us kids. Daddy was always working in the fields or working on the old car that was always broken down. Momma was trying to get food or cook what food we had, so she always was busy. Little Granny became our caregiver, and we liked it that way.

Little Granny was one of the most important people in my life, and she continued to influence me long after she left this world.

Momma and we girls worked in the fields, and we better have earned all we could or we were going to get in bad trouble. Curtis would just ride around with Daddy on the tractor or truck and not have to work all day.

Daddy would tie a knot in the middle of Curtis cotton sack, so Curtis was able to pick as many sacks as the rest of us. We had to pick full sacks for the same credit with Daddy.

We all resented Curtis and Daddy for that, but they did not seem to care. Momma dare not say anything, or she would take a beating from Daddy and it would not change a thing. All of us girls would cry at night from of being exhausted, hungry, and having bad blisters on our hands and feet from the hot dry fields.

Curtis would laugh and make faces at us when we cried about the blisters. Curtis is like a blister; he shows up after the work is done!

We were just little kids but, we had to work like grown ups all day, without food. If we were hungry we better like whatever we were picking or it was going to be a long and hungry day. But, don't get caught eating the harvest too often or you would have to pay for eatin' it.

When we were cutting hops or picking cotton we would have to go hungry most of the day. Momma would pick some greens or something, but that would be it. I got so sick of eating greens as a kid that when I grew up, I could not even stand the smell of them cooking.

Sometimes, Daddy was able to trade stuff in town, or around the camp for different food, and that always was nice.

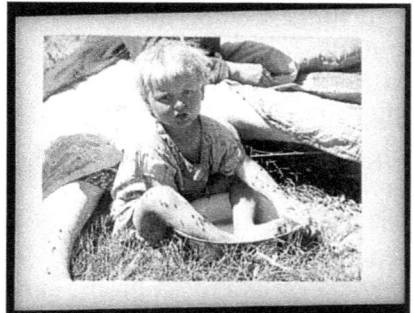

Daddy did the best when he traded peaches. Most of the communities were small, and they traded for them because the peaches were so sweet and juicy.

We would keep some of the real nice

ones hid in the grass along the edge of the field, and then we would go back at dark and retrieve them. The next day he would be off to town to see what he could get for them in trade.

We knew it was wrong to steal, but when you are hungry it does not seem to matter as much. The things I was willing to do for food, I would not do for anything else.

When it came to do the heavy work in the fields, it mainly fell upon just a couple of us kids. Curtis was riding in Daddy's lap on the tractor. Midge was sick, and could only do a little bit before she was crying. Momma was trying to watch out after all of us kids, and work at the same time.

That left it to Donnie, me and Little Granny, who could only do so much - she only weighed about a hundred pounds, and was so skinny she didn't even make a shadow on the ground. If we girls didn't earn enough for the day, we got a beating.

Bella was little and spent most of the time just playing and running around.

Donnie and I ended up doing most of the field work because the others did not care, and always talked about leaving as soon as they could find a ride out of town. I'm not sure where they thought they would get away too, but they always talked about it. All day I had to listen to all the stories about leaving and what they would do when they were on their own. Boy, did they get a lesson on that!

They would leave, and pretty soon they were back - all beat up from whoever the last boyfriend was, and hungry to boot.

The worst was picking cotton. There was no shade, hot and dry, bent over all day and dragging a ten foot long cloth sack that got heavier by the handful. We dragged it along between those skinny rows with the sharp vines picking at our ankles and arms, swatting flies and keeping an eye-out for snakes. I hated that work, and I was made to do it for as long as I can remember, from sunup to sundown.

Picking cotton paid three dollars for 100 pounds delivered to the truck. I remember dragging that cotton sack to the truck. The men weighing and loading would comment on how I was able to drag that sack weighing more than I did. It made me feel good about what I had done but it was so hard to understand why I had to work so hard. I did not get any of the money so I had no incentive to do more than I felt was my duty.

Daddy sometimes would cut firewood for the railroad company and we had to pitch in there, too. If we had a couple days wait for cotton, or whatever we were picking at the time, we would cut and stack firewood next to the railroad tracks.

Daddy was so strong in his right arm because he could saw wood with just that one hand. He used his stump some to push, but when he pulled that saw blade back, it was all right arm. Other men would sometimes stop and watch Daddy cutting wood and shake their heads at what he could do. All of us girls would be running around picking up what they were cutting and making big stacks, so we could finish what he expected for the day and go home.

We would watch the other men cut wood and if we had a chance to grab a piece or two of their wood, we would do it. I think they knew we were doing it but were afraid to say anything because of Daddy and his tough reputation. We would make five dollars for cutting and stacking wood all day. That was good money.

The railroad only needed so much wood at each location, so whoever cut the most in the shortest period of time made the most money. I think most of what we were cutting was eucalyptus and it was hard wood to cut, and heavy to carry so we rolled the pieces over to the stack, and we all worked together to lift the big pieces.

We lived in a lot of roadside camps with big eucalyptus groves. The smell of them will never leave my mind. The rustling of those long leaves and the shade they gave us was welcome. The bark was good for starting fires and the wood burned for a long time so we didn't have to have that much of it on hand.

I also can tell you that it makes one heck of a switch for getting your butt spanked. If we were to get a spanking Daddy would tell us to go get a switch from the tree, and we better bring a good one. We had to pick one that would not break when he spanked us with it or he would make us go pick another one and start the spanking all over again. That's just how it was in those days.

Those green eucalyptus switches are pretty tough, and I guess it made us pretty tough too. I got to the point where I didn't even cry when he spanked me. It wasn't long before he quit spanking me, and would just yell at me as punishment. I was not in much trouble anyway, and Daddy knew how hard I worked. He let me get away with some stuff, just a good finger waving and a stern, "Betty Girl" and I was changing whatever he did not like.

It was kind of hard to see the other kids get a whipping, but it meant that it would probably spare me for the day. I would just look away and find something else to do.

Once Daddy got on you it seemed like he watched you like a hawk the rest of the day. We tried real hard to not be the one he was mad at for the day because you could do nothing right after that.

Work was short most of the time and food was always in short supply. We found other ways to make a little money. Little Granny would take us along the road to pick up glass. We could make a dollar a day selling what we found, and it gave us something to do besides sit at the cabin and wait to get in trouble with our folks.

We never made much because other families were doing the same thing, but it was something for us to do. It was an adventure. Little Granny would try to find something to talk about, or a way to teach us something as we walked along those roads. Everything was a lesson, from the kinds of birds we would see and how to cook them, to the kinds of cars passing on the roadway beside us, and how rich you had to be to own one.

We would talk about the kind of work rich people did and how it would be to live like that. It always made its way around to going to school and getting a good education.

Little Granny was pretty smart you see, she knew a lot about the world. She could see what was going on around her, and she knew how to survive. She said it was her job to teach us how to survive too. She was fun to learn from.

She taught me how to use my imagination. A grain tower next to the rail tracks became a castle, and we were living in it. An empty building became a modern home, and we lived in it with servants who would bring us all the food and cold drinks we could ever want.

Little Granny said, "We should never stop dreaming and never stop living for our dreams. Dreams renew hope. Without hope we are doomed to die a slow miserable death - a kind of death that works on your mind and body, every moment of your existence. Dreams last a lifetime, and are lived out in a moment. Take time to dream in this moment and it will be true." I loved to listen to Little Granny.

I remember her telling all kinds of stories about the Great Depression and how hope is all she had left at times. There was no work, no food, no home and Grandpa died so no husband either. At times she must have felt so alone.

She said it was her dreams that kept her going each day. Most of them must have been for us kids because I don't remember her ever asking for a thing for herself. She was unselfish, and maybe thought she would never live her dreams, so she tried to help us kids live ours, even if it was just for a moment. Maybe we were her dream, the Lord only knows.

I know we had it hard and it must have been very hard for Momma and Daddy to watch us struggle so much. As I got older, I could not begin to imagine what it must have been like to know your kids had to go to bed hungry, not having eaten more than a couple peaches or some greens for the whole day.

I am not sure what it looked like to be hungry, but I sure as heck knew what it felt like to be hungry. I wanted to make sure I never had to see my kids hungry when I grew up and had my own family. I was willing to do whatever, and to whoever I had to do it, so my kids would not have to experience that pain. You see, hunger does not just affect your belly; it is equally hard on your mind and your soul.

I don't care who you are, hunger is hard and it must have been what caused me to never quit as I grew up, and I mean never.

I would close my eyes at night and could hear my belly growling for food. I could hear all the kids' bellies doing the same thing. Imagine listening to your own; now think about hearing all your kids' their bellies doing it, too.

Hope for tomorrow is all I had those days, hope that I would not have to go hungry another day.

Sometimes it was best to just go to sleep. I would keep my mind busy until sleep swept me away to my dreams.

One of my dreams at the time was to get out of those hot cotton fields. It was killing my little body and my soul, having to work like the grown men I worked beside. I knew this was not the way it would be for me the rest of my life, I needed more.

We were in California picking cotton when we got word the government was providing a train ride from where we were in Bakersfield to Stockton for the tomato harvest. Pickers were needed right away and the wages were the highest they had been in years for the tomato harvest.

I don't remember the reason, but we didn't have a car at the time, so the offer for free transportation was too good to pass up. Daddy signed us up for the work that day. We didn't have much, so we rolled things up and left for Stockton within a couple days.

We were loaded up in those train cars like a bunch of cattle, but no one seemed to care. Everybody was smiling and talking loud like we were going to a party. The trip was to take all day, we were told, and there would be no stops.

A box of food was put on with us, and a man with the farm we were going to rode along in the train car with us. We all sat on the floor and listened as he told everybody about the jobs and how things would be there. I was so excited about the train ride, I don't remember much about what he told us. I just remember looking out those big open doors and watching the world go by faster than I had ever seen before.

We finally did get to that box of food; it was bread and avocados, that's it.

Because it's all we had, we made avocado sandwiches. Curtis just sat there looking at the avocados like it was something he had never seen before; come to think of it, it may have been the first time he ever really noticed what avocados were. Anyway, there was no way he was going to eat an avocado sandwich so Momma took the avocado off of the bread and he ate plain old bread. I got his piece of avocado and ate every bite of it. I still like them to this day. Every time I eat one I think of that day, and I laugh.

21

We got to the camp in Stockton late that day, and they drove us right to the cabins. We were assigned our cabin and they handed out buckets for the picking that was to start the next day. Daddy got a picking bucket for each of us. He handed each of us one and we sat on it as he told us what assignment would be ours for the next day's work. We all knew the work would be hard and it was hot, but that didn't matter because we were all hungry and the picking job would give us money for much needed food.

The field we were to work in was on a small hill just outside town. I could see the town from our cabin door. That night it was so hot you could hardly breathe, we were taking turns sitting in the doorway hoping for a little breeze. As I watched the lights from town that night I wondered what it was like to live there. I always asked myself what 'I would be' if I lived in this or that town as we worked and traveled through them.

I was getting a little older and was starting to wonder about the towns we passed through, working for a few weeks and then moving on again. I still look at the lights of a town I am passing through and wonder the same thing; what is it like to live here, are the people nice, and is there a good school and a big library. Why do people live here, what is so special that they stay here? I always wonder why people live where they do. I guess that will never change for me.

There were ten of us, seven kids, my parents and Granny. We were a family. We had our problems, but we worked and lived in one of the most difficult times in modern history. I don't know how we did it, and I don't know how other families did it but we did. We had to. We had to live for the next generation; we had to make it better so they would not have to experience and suffer like we did.

Many of the lessons I learned as a kid I have used as adult so I would not make the same mistake twice. Sometimes when I talk to my brother and sisters it is like time has stood still. It sounds like it did when we were kids. I don't know why it is but it is. They say the same things they always have and in the same way. It is like I know what and how they will say things even before they say them. Some things never change, maybe it's not supposed to. I did not give them my hard earned money then and I can hear it coming in the conversation now, just before they tell me how much they could use some help with a small loan, one I know will never be repaid.

As I think about it, I wonder why it is that we let family treat us the way they do. They are my brother and sisters, not my rulers. They do not own me nor should I allow them to control me in any way. Why do we allow family to continue to treat us the same way when we get older? We are no longer in the same house and no longer required to accept the old circumstance.

I have tried to figure out how it is that the same little kids, who always fought over the stupid things, grow older and continue to fight over the stupid things! Why do I argue with them over things that I never do with my friends and neighbors? Why do we still have the same anger with each other as adults? Why do I still care about the same things as I did when we were young kids fighting over these things? Are they unresolved arguments? Is it my attempt to recover from the hurt they caused me as a child? Why do we continue to challenge our family members in ways we don't challenge anyone else?

I wonder if we think that because we are family, we have some right or ownership of other family members and, their choices in life.

Now that we are adults, I have to let go of the problems of my childhood completely, or I will never be independent from them.

My youth has to suffer this loss. That part of me has to die for the new part of me to grow and prosper. The independent "me" wants to come alive, but it is being held down by the old me, my childhood.

I must learn to accept my family for who they really are, not who I want them to be. We lived in the same cabin and put on countless miles down those same dusty hot roads as kids. They had their own experiences in the same moment as me, in the same space and time as me; but they were separate personal experiences for each of us and it now means different things to each of us.

See, every person has a right to their own experience and opinion about events, even if it is at the same time and place as yours. We must accept each person as an individual. Yes, even if it is one of my family. We were so close in many ways and so far apart in others. Funny huh?

Thank you Lord for finally liberating me from all the burdens of my youth, and delivering me freedom from my family, freedom I have longed for. It took me many years to understand that all of the trouble I was having with my family members was trouble I was allowing them to create for me.

Until I stopped trying to decide who and what they needed to be, I couldn't separate myself from whom they wanted to make me. I just want to live to my own potential, in sync with the world I desire.

I was afraid to let go. I was afraid to move on. I guess it was not as bad as it seemed now that I look back, and have survived it. We are family. Some things never change. We should be glad of that.

CHAPTER FOUR

On Daddy's Shoulders

The first time I remember going to school I would have been about six years old that would have made it about 1940.

We were living in Visalia, California at the time and living up on "Rocky Hill," just outside town. The camp at the time was no different than all the others. I got so sick of living like this, but that was our existence. Another cabin in another camp filled with hungry and desperate people. We all had some things in common; we were hungry, always tired and always looking for a way to get needed food or money.

I think everybody kept a pretty close eye on things, because if someone was not watching out for what little we had, someone else would take it.

Little Granny kept watch for us all the time, and she would not let anyone get to close to our things. She could get pretty riled up if she needed to because she was intent on watching out for her family. She was a regular bird dog.

The great San Joaquin Valley was where we spent most of our season working the cotton fields and citrus groves. We picked up olives when we needed other work, but the pay was not as good, and Daddy said he hated the stain it left on his fingers because it turned them all black just like walnuts do.

I wanted to go to school like the other kids in the camp. The school bus would stop down at the bottom of the hill every morning, and I would watch the kids get on and off. I waited for them to come home in the afternoon and could see the bus driving along that long winding road up to the camp.

The other kids would tell stories about what they learned that day, and I was fascinated. I wanted to learn. I was hungry for the world and what was in it. A world outside of the one I was living in that was hungry and desperate.

My sisters would go to school some of the time but they didn't seem to care about school. If they stayed home, they had to work in the field with Daddy, so school was a place to get rest, not education.

I think Donnie was hurt by the things other school kids said to her because we were poor, and the old worn out cloths and shoes made her a target. Donnie was dark skinned and had dark hair. She looked like a Native

American Indian and the Indians did not have a good reputation with local farmers, so she was teased a lot and would rather stay home and work then have to listen to the insults.

Midge had Polio and got teased because of her odd looking legs. Her legs were crooked and skinny; she could not walk without braces or someone to help hold her up. She hurt a lot and it made her cry so she didn't really want to go to school and have to suffer without someone to help care for her pain.

Midge and I had the same size feet, so we shared shoes most of the time. If she wanted to go to school, I was left without shoes for the day and would have to help Momma work the edges of the field in the soft dirt. The bottoms of my feet were tough as leather at an early age and stayed that way all my life.

We had been living up and down the lush San Joaquin Valley for several months, and we regulars drove by the local school when we were in town for supplies. I asked Daddy about going to school with the other kids but never really got an answer - it usually was just a stern look and nothing more.

Daddy believed in school but knew what the other girls had to go through with being teased and,didn't want"Betty Girl" to have to deal with it, too. I only had two sets of clothes that were passed down to me by my older sister Donnie. She got them used from a local church that helped the Fruit Tramps, as we called, when they passed through town during the last harvest season-so to say they were a little worn would be an understatement.

I remember a sign posted in front of a church as we came into Visalia that read, 'Fruit Tramps welcome, stop on in.' Well, we always did because we could pick up some clothes, and every now and then we could get a pair of used shoes. The shoes never fit right and were always a size or two, too big. They did provided some protection from the hot or wet ground, and because they were so big, it easy to slip your feet in and out of, too.

Those same churches, Nazarene I believe, always had some food in a box for all of us who were making our way in for harvest, and they were always nice to us kids. I remember one lady there; I was only a young girl, about six, and had nothing more than a dirty face, bare feet and old worn out clothing. We were getting ready to leave, and she called Momma over to her and handed her the prettiest blanket I had ever seen. She pointed to me and then gave Momma a hug. I did get that blanket from Momma and, kept it for most of my childhood. I don't remember how old I was when I stopped using it, but I do remember it was worn plum out.

That blanket provided me many nights of warmth and comfort in pretty hostile environments-of-living in cabins and on the side of the fields. I would wrap myself up in it and remember someone cared about me. I would wrap up my sister Midge in it too, and tell her she would be okay, like that blanket had some power to stop the hurt. Midge cried a lot of tears in that blanket. I wish I could tell that lady thank you, and let her know how special that simple gift was to me for so many years. I don't remember her name, but love her for that act of kindness to me.

Midge used to tell me I should go to school and encouraged me to be smart. She told me she would help with the school work so I could pass the grades. We would talk about math, history and reading for hours at a time. I wanted to go to school, because I wanted have an education and not have to spend the rest of my life working in those dusty fields.

Even as a small child, I recognized the difference of how we lived compared to others. When we went into town, and I looked at all those houses and wondered what that must be like, living in one place, going to school every day and having my own nice clothes and shoes. I wanted to look like the other kids. I wanted to be one of the other kids; how come I had to be poor?

When Daddy did finally let me start going to school some, I would wonder if today would be the day we would leave, yet again. The work is done and it is time to move to the next crop or field, or Daddy got fired because they found out he had only one hand. Sometimes I would get picked up at school and off we were on the road again without being able to say bye to my friends. It happened so often that friends didn't really matter anymore.

I thought, how do I get close to people when I'm in constant fear of leaving, never to see them again, or at least not until next year if we ended up back at that field? Most of the time, I did not get to advance in school grades like the local kids because my attendance was so infrequent, I fell behind in the studies.

It always was hard and a little embarrassing to return to a school and find the kids who were in the same class as me the year before, are now in a class ahead of me. They would see me and sometimes make fun of me and call me stupid.

Sometimes, I just couldn't take it anymore and would prefer to stay home from school, and work in the fields. Of course Daddy was okay with it because I was a good worker and it meant more money at the end of the week for the family.

Momma wished I would go to school, but understood why I didn't want to go. Some kids were so cruel. I was not going to cry though, because I wanted to be strong. So, I just put that emotion into working hard and wanted people to just stay out of my way. Momma would try to make sure I had something to do that made me feel important in those times. Sometimes I felt very alone.

It was hard for me to understand - I was just a kid and I already felt different then the local kids. My clothes were different. I lived in a cabin and not a house. We used an outhouse and did not have running water in the cabin. The only electricity was one light hanging from the ceiling. Many times we could see right through the walls to the outside because of the cracks between the boards on the walls.

I sounded different; the way I talked, my accent was different. We were from Oklahoma; Okies or Arkies as we were called by some. Usually it was simply; fruit tramp.

My clothes were too big or too small because we had to wear what the other kids threw away or donated.

I never owned anything new, never bought a dress at a store and never had a new pair of shoes. Most of the time we had to wear boy's pants and shirts because it was better for working in the fields then a dress. We did not have different clothes for work and school, they were always the same.

If I remember right, at times, I only had one set of anything, and all of the girls had to share whatever we had.

In spite of all this, I wanted to learn and be smart. I wanted to overcome all the teasing and differences I felt at school. I wanted to be like the other kids and not feel poor or like an outsider all the time. I would try to go to school and get books, or go to a library and get them so I could read and study on my own.

As I look back, I think how funny that sounds, teach myself things I didn't know. I did not always learn a lot about whatever I was reading, but it gave me confidence that I could learn on my own and helped me to not feel like the other kids were superior to me.

Momma would help me, but the older girls didn't want to go to school and didn't even want to read with me or help me learn. Sometimes Midge would but she was the only one who would try to help.

Momma would tell me about things I was reading - she seemed so smart at times, and she was just overwhelmed with all the kids. Taking care of Midge, was at times a full time job, and trying to keep us fed and out of trouble was another full time job; she didn't have much time to help me study.

Momma had several full time jobs, keeping the family alive and fed were the two most important. Momma was no different than all the mothers of the world who have so much work to do for the family that they seem to forget about themselves. Thank God for mothers!

As I look back, I'm not sure if Momma knew the stuff I was asking, or if she just made stuff up. Either way it helped me to believe in myself.

Some of the stories she would tell, helped me to dream about what I could become. I knew when I got older I was not going to be poor and have to feel like everybody was superior to me.

Stories of other places and other countries and how they lived was exciting to a young girl looking for a place to be somebody accepted and respected.

In my dreams, I could be whoever I wanted, live anywhere I wanted and choose who I lived with. School and history books created another life for me, a life where I had nice clothes and plenty of food, the kind of food I liked, and no beans!

I loved history, it let me imagine my own world that I desperately needed and wanted a world different than the one in which I was imprisoned.

I loved listening to stories about history, about the settlers and pioneers of this country. I loved the perseverance and how tough they were. They had to overcome great difficulty and change their world to make it better. They had to fight against those who wanted to conquer and control them. The pioneers were people who were willing to fight for independence in the world they had to share.

Those people wanted to make a place where everybody had a chance. They accepted that people have different talents and interests and the place they wanted not only had to allow that to exist, but had to support one's chance to develop. People had to be respected and listened to because nothing else would be accepted. They were smart, tough and acted together as one voice for freedom.

History was my escape, my dream, my new world. I heard Daddy say how we had to live in the world we were given and our dreams were no more than dreams, we had to accept what we had and who we were.

I remember telling Daddy one time, that's not a dream then, dreams are the place where I can be whatever I want; I don't remember if Daddy said anything back to me, he just let me have my dream of dreams, it was what gave me hope for my tomorrow.

It's funny that I remember that so well. We were living close by the railroad tracks working on a cotton field, hoeing rows and, the cotton gin was just in the distance. We could see and hear the trains coming and going all the time and a lot of the time they came and went at night.

I could look at that cotton gin standing up tall in those flat fields and think of it as a castle. It was fun to dream like that just to get away, if even for a moment, from the heat and wind that was so constant.

That old wooden gin looked to be a hundred feet tall to me. There always was dust blowing out of it, and I pretended it was smoke, like it was on fire. I would play out how I would climb up and save people from that burning tower and the whole town would hoist me on their shoulders to celebrate me, just like the pictures I had seen in the books of those returning from battle victorious.

Castles, and saving people from evil kings were my dreams and they gave me a place to belong, to be equal or even better. It seems like every time I saw the tall towers along the tracks and fields, I would allow myself to go to those same dreams and dream them again and again. I never got tired of those dreams.

As I lay awake at night I would hear the train whistles and think about where the train was going, still do. I knew it was taking a load of goods somewhere I had never been before, a place I could only imagine in my dreams.

The sound of the whistle became the stop where I got on board. I would be bound for some other place, a better place. I could hear the whistle in the distance and start to wonder who was on that train; I wondered where it was going and what it would be like when it got to its destination.

Trying to escape what I was living and, creating better things in my mind was God's way of letting me escape from it. Hope was alive and well in my dreams, still is today. We should never stop dreaming or give up on hope.

If you ever listen to the train whistles at night and wondered where the train is going, who is going, and how the adventure will turn out, you will understand how comforting the sound is to me. It reminds me of another time - a time when I dreamed the trains were all going to someplace special. They were going to a place where I wanted to go, to get away from the very difficult existence I was living.

I never want to live in a place where there are no trains or whistles in the night. Those memories whistle me home, home to my family and my childhood, as difficult as it was; I have mostly fond memories of family.

As I look back at my life, I think in terms of those special markers that we remember with each big event in our lives -smells, music, and the things we feared. Do you do the same thing when you remember back to your childhood?

Certain things happen at times in your life that shape the rest of your life, even though we do not know how important it will be for us later on in life. So we just go into them for what it serves us at that time, not thinking of our future.

Well, it is no different than the first day I remember going to school. We were in Visalia and living way out next to the field we were working in.

I remember asking to go to school every day. Every time we went to town and would pass that church that helped fruit tramps, we would stop and Momma would ask if they had any dresses my size. She would look through the pile of clothes on the table for something that might fit me.

I'm not sure, but I think those ladies knew I wanted to go to school and Momma was looking for a dress and shoes I could wear. Well, as I remember, we went there for the third time and Momma asked to look through the pile when the ladies said, "Oh, we got something here that might work for that girl of yours. It just came in today and we put it back thinking it was perfect for Betty."

That lady handed Momma the paper bag, and she took a quick look inside. I can still remember the look on mamma's face when she looked in; she looked up at me, and I could see tears in her eyes. I knew something was going on because Mamma just grabbed me up as she walked us to the door; she kept thanking the ladies as we went out the door to the truck where Daddy and Donnie were waiting.

It wasn't until we got home later that day that Momma showed me what was in that bag. It was a pretty dress and matching shoes. Those shoes did not have a scratch on them. Momma said they looked 'brand new' and she let me try them on that night after supper.

I was so excited to put that dress on, and I couldn't quit looking at the shoes. Me and Midge each slipped on the shoes and would look at each other like we were a princess or something. We had never had such a pretty pair of shoes in our life. We kept talking about how pretty the dress was, how it would fit and what each of us would look like in it. We lost ourselves in the dream for hours.

We went to the water pump out front and got a bucket to wash up in right after supper. Each of us washed like we were trying to rub a layer of skin off. We wanted to be so clean for that dress, not wanting to get even one spot of dirt on it. It was the prettiest dress I had ever seen.

Well, after we got done scrubbing ourselves and washing our hair, I remember walking back to the cabin, I had to keep looking down to see if I was even touching the ground. This was the nicest dress I had ever seen, and it was mine.

Momma spent the next hour brushing the tangles out of my hair; I guess it had been awhile since we had done that. There was no need to brush it all out to go play in the hot dry dirt in the cotton fields, but was absolutely necessary, if I wanted to put on that pretty dress.

Well, we finely got my hair brushed, the whole time I was just staring at that dress all laid out on the edge of that old bed. I was shaking when Momma held it down for me to step into. I had never felt that way before and for that matter, I don't remember ever wearing a dress, it was always boy's pants before.

Donnie was mad because she did not get one that would fit her too, so she went outside so she didn't have to see me put it on. Midge sat right there and kept looking at me with a bright smile. She was so happy for me.

I finally stood still long enough for Mamma to give it a pull up. All of a sudden I was wearing the most beautiful dress in the world. Momma hooked the buttons in back and kept twisting that thing like she was trying to work it up on me. She was pulling it up, and I was grabbing the bottom and pulling down so my bottom didn't show. We all started laughing and giggling, we were having the time of our lives.

Daddy was shaking his head not understanding what this meant to me and Momma - he never said a word the whole time. He just stood there smiling and watching.

The shoes were sitting on the dusty old floor as I stepped into them,I felt like a princess for the first time in my life.

I couldn't help myself. I started dancing around and spinning in circles. Midge went to singing and Momma was crying. We were a mess.

Donnie came back in to see what all the commotion was about and started laughing at us like we were crazy. I guess she forgot about not getting a dress and shoes and just wanted to celebrate with us. We didn't hesitate to let her.

It was one of the happiest days and fondest memories of my childhood. I never felt that way again about a dress and shoe's the rest of my life.

That is the dress and shoes I wore to school the very first day. I got up early and Momma helped me wash my face and brush my hair. She helped me put on that dress,and I slipped into those pretty shoes. I was so excited to have them on again and so excited to go to school for the first time.

I thought I would walk down to the bus stop with the other kids and ride that old yellow bus to the school in town. Boy was I surprised when Daddy told me he was taking me to school for my first day. He said he had taken the other girls for their first day and he wanted to do the same thing for his Betty Girl.

Daddy borrowed the truck from the ranch foreman and pulled it around to the front of the cabin like he was driving his princess to the ball.

I remember Momma helping me up in the seat and worrying it was going to get my dress dirty, so she wiped it off with her shirt sleeve to make a clean spot. I climbed in, and off we went to town. I remember looking out of the window of that old truck wondering what it would be like, going to school like the other kids. I was as nervous as I was excited, I couldn't tell the difference between the two.

Daddy didn't look over at me the whole trip. He just looked out of the windshield and had a smile on his face. It was such a different experience for me to have this chance and share it with my daddy.

We arrived at the school, and I was ready to jump out and run to class. I'm not sure what I was thinking because I had never been to that school and had no idea where my classroom was at.

Daddy somehow kept me from jumping out of the truck; he took my hand and reached under the seat pulling out an old cigar box. The box was old and worn out. The edges were all worn down and the lid was barely hanging on. He reached into it and shuffled some old papers around as if he were looking for something.

I asked him what the box was and after a short pause he said, "It's my Box of Secrets," then he put his finger up to his lips and said, "Shhhhhhh-hhh."

He then pulled out a shiny penny and handed it to me. He said, "Put this in your shoe and it will bring you good luck." I gave him a big smile and a brief hug and in my shoe it went.

We got out of that truck and started to walk into the school when all of a sudden Daddy just lifted me up onto his shoulders. Wow, he had never done that before. I wasn't sure what to do, so I just hung on. I felt so big and it was very special. I felt my Daddy's love and happiness for me at that moment like never before.

It is one of the most cherished moments of my childhood and it has given me much happiness in my later years remembering back on that day, that moment. It was all I had believed it would be, and I was living it.

I did go to school that fall day in Visalia, for the very first time. It was everything I expected it to be and I would not change that for anything. I remember that first day like it was yesterday. I can still smell the classroom and see the supplies across the counter space for each of us. The small table and chairs all in rows so neat and orderly.

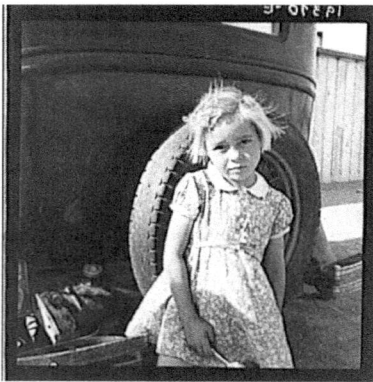

We each found a seat and made a name tag, the teacher pinned it on us so she would know our names. I can't tell you how I felt hearing her say, "Betty Jean" does this or that. It was one of the few days in my childhood I felt like I belonged. I was like all the other kids!

The teacher had us sit back at our table after standing in front of the class and telling our name to the others. She gave each of us a big piece of paper. We all looked at each other wondering what we were to do with it, and we giggled as we waited for her to tell us what we would be doing.

I was part of the class, just like all the other kids. We were all the same but all different too. I can still see the look on everybody's face.

She then set a tray of blue colored paint in the middle of our table and said, "Wait, I will show you what we are going to do in just a minute - wait now."

As we all waited and watched, she placed her own paper down on the table, dipped her hand into the tray of paint covering the palm of her hand with blue paint and then she placed it on that sheet of paper. Just as quickly as she put her hand on the paper, she lifted it up, holding her hand up in the air.

"See what we are going to do. We are making our print on the paper for our family. Now let's all do the same." Take your time, she declared, and then she walked around the room as we worked and watched the others do the same as she had done.

I remember I waited for some of the others to do their print first so I could see what they were doing and how it worked. It was important for me because I wanted mine to be perfect.

I did make a print, and I remember giving it to Daddy when he picked me up that day after school.

Daddy smiled real big and then folded it in half before he put it in his jacket pocket.

Every minute of that day and all of the sights and sounds of it echo in my mind as I have grown much older - almost eighty now.

That was one of the days in my young life when I felt loved. It was a day when I felt like all the kids accepted me, I felt normal. It was a day when I felt like my parents really loved me and were proud of me. I did not want this day to end because I felt like I never had before.

On that day there was no hate, no division, and no difference. If not for the photo I would not have remembered the color of the dress, the shoes or the school building where I first fulfilled my dream. The name of the school is long forgotten and the names of the other kids have since passed from memory. I remember little of all those things that seemed to mean so much to me as a child.

What remains is the day my Daddy loved me, without fault or consequence. The love I felt for him, and his love for me, I knew it was real. My first love was my father, "Daddy," I love him and that will never change.

I had few opportunities to go to school as I grew up and to stay at one school for an entire year never happened. I was the kid who showed up at school and just as I was getting settled into the routine and making friends, we were on the move again. You remember that kid don't you? What was their name, what did they look like. Do you only remember the old clothing and worn out shoes?

It was very difficult to learn in those conditions and, if it were not for Momma and Little Granny, we would have had the opportunity to go to school and receive even less education then we did.

Both Momma and Little Granny were great teachers and we learned as we went. They used all kinds of things to teach us math and reading as we traveled across this land.

CHAPTER FIVE

On The Road

More Oklahomans reach Calif. via the cotton fields of Ariz.

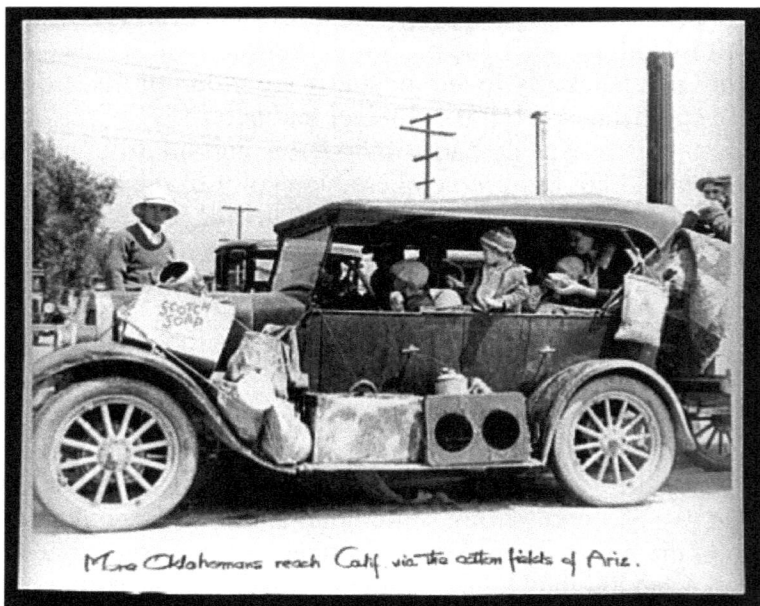

I still can remember how I felt each time we packed to hit the road for another year of tramping. I would start thinkin' of the hot dusty roads ahead, and the endless hours of being cramped up in the back of whatever car Daddy had that year.

Long days of travel with few stops and little food, drinking warm water from the canvass water bag slung on front of the car's radiator and being afraid to ask if we could stop so we could go to the bathroom.

Sleeping on canvas tarps with one blanket to cover up with in the tramp camps along the highway, and wishing I could just stay in one place for awhile.

Every year, Daddy seemed to have a knack for buying the worst car in the county. He would buy an old car and then spend the next month working on it. It seemed that each day brought another trip to the wrecking yard for parts and advice on how to do the impossible with as little money as possible.

He would work on that old car, cuss, quit and start all over again at least three times a day.

One year it was an old Hudson that would take us down the never-ending ribbon of highway. When he drove that thing up in front of the little house we were living in at the time in Gentry, Arkansas, I remember Momma saying, "Why does he do that, does he hate me?"

That old car was smoking and making noise so loud you could hear it clear across the creek up at Fox Trot Ridge. Momma was embarrassed to have that old car out in front of our cabin –and that was interesting because we had the most run down, drafty cabin around. Daddy would tell people it was so full of holes that the wind didn't even slow down as it blew through.

Other times, after Daddy bought the cheapest car he could find, he'd start scouting old broken down cars for parts. I think he would buy cars he knew he could get parts for because of all the ones like it we saw along the road and in nearby fields.

Out Daddy would go, late at night, and look for parts while most people were sleeping, hoping to get the parts without having to pay for them. I remember Daddy telling us to keep quiet and stay inside when people would show up at our cabin asking about missing car parts. He always said he got the needed parts with the "five finger discount" system. It was years later before I understood what that meant.

Daddy would argue with them when they would try to look under the hood of that old car. As soon as they did, the fight would be on. Daddy could whop just about any man that came looking, and that would be the end of it. I don't remember Daddy ever giving anybody anything back; he would put the part on the car a couple days later, just in case the cops came by looking for him and any missing car parts. If anyone would ask what year his old car was he would start with a laugh and say something like; it's a thirty-three, thirty-four, thirty-nine, forty-one, Chevy.

I don't know how he made all those different parts work, but he somehow did.

I remember Daddy called the police "a bunch of pencil necks." He never had any use for the police. He said all they did was interfere in his business. He said the law was for sale, and it was for the rich and of course, that did not include us.

So came another year of leaving my few friends, and whatever stray dog I had befriended. I used to hide things in hollowed-out tree stumps and by creek beds because I knew there was no room to bring any toys or 'treasures.' I could only hope we would return to that area again so I could find my cache another year. My treasures never amounted to much, some colored rocks I picked up in the creek or some old toy I had found and kept hidden so the other kids wouldn't tear it up or take it away. I would hide them so I could keep them for myself forever.

I learned to hold on to things with a pretty loose grip. It seemed like everything was to be mine for a short time - a season, and then they were left behind - only mine to keep in my memories.

Many friends I made I knew I would never see again. It was hard for me as a little kid, but I somehow managed to do it year-after-year. After awhile, I even stopped crying when we would leave. That was just how it was, and crying never changed a thing, so I just got hardened to it and never really got to close too the other children. They were playmates for today that was all.

One of the last things we did before we left was to empty the grass out of our mattress cover. When Momma told us to take the mattress out and pull all the stuffing grass out, we knew we were leaving very soon.

Each of us had a job to do before leaving, and sometimes mine was to empty the cover. It was not hard to do, it was just kind of dusty and it made me itch.

We would carry that cover all folded up in the bottom of the car until we were going to stay for somewhere for awhile. It would have to be more than a few days, because it took us that long to fill the cover mattress with grass.

It was nice to have soft grass to sleep on. As soon as we could, we would start looking for tall grass near where we were working. Momma called it scouting. Scouting was another word for more work but we were kids and the word somehow made it fun, besides, until we had enough grass to fill the cover we were sleeping on the hard floor.

At the end of each day, we would cut an arm full of grass and each of us kids would carry it back to where we were staying. It was kind of fun to stuff that tall grass into the mattress cover and climb in and out of it as we filled it up. We learned how to stuff it in there so when we lay upon it, the grass wouldn't poke us. It took some skill to lay all that grass in there, one way and then the other, back and forth all the way out to the end where we would tie it closed.

Some of the cabins we stayed in had a mattress on the bed, filled with cotton or cotton seed. Momma and Little Granny would sleep on that one, and all of us kids, and Daddy, would lay the grass-filled mattress, on the floor. Each of us had a blanket for a cover, and it wasn't too bad, especially for kids. It did not seem to be as hot on the floor as it was up on the bed, so I think we had the better place, anyway.

The cold was more trouble than the heat for me. I didn't have other clothes I could put on, and only had a coat some of the time, so cold was harder to fend off.

I remember one time when we were in Ruidoso, New Mexico sometime in early April. The temperatures at night had been down in the twenties, and the wind was blowing every day. It was bitter cold in our old car that had more holes in it then a minnow bucket.

We were broke down, again, and had just been kicked out of a small town where we were on the side of the road, trying to fix the car. The police stopped long enough to tell Daddy get all his tramp kids back in the car and head for the City Limit sign.

Daddy had some choice things to say to them. I don't remember everything he said, but I do remember the police telling Daddy to head out now, or he would be arrested. I think Daddy told him, "We are not vagrants, we are broke down, as soon as I can fix it were leaving."

Daddy somehow got the old Hudson started, and off we went with Daddy mad as Heck, and Momma telling him to just drive on to the next town so we could stay there for the night. Well, we only made it a short distance, just out of town when the old Hudson gave it up, a snap and a couple pops and we coasted to the side of the road.

This type of breakdown was a reoccurring event my entire childhood.

I remember looking out the window and there was not a tree in sight. The wind was blowing, and night was coming on quick. It looked like it would be another very cold night huddled up in the back seat of the car with all of us fighting for the few blankets we had.

Daddy was out with the hood up working on the car while the rest of us watched from inside to see if we were staying or going. He worked and cussed.

I heard Daddy call out to Momma, "Looks like I'm going to jail, a police car just pulled up behind us." All of us kids were scrunched up under the covers, and dared not look out; as we knew Daddy would be mad and would yell at us if we said a word.

I could hear Daddy talking to somebody and then Daddy said, "You kids look here, get on out from those covers and look here, the police want to see ya."

We were afraid, so I had to be the first to look out. One-by-one, we stuck our heads out from under the covers until all our faces were looking right at Daddy with the policeman standing next to him, looking in. The policeman was shaking his head, and I heard him tell Daddy, "Get 'em out and back here to my car." Right then, I knew Daddy was going to jail, and it looked like the rest of us were going with him.

Momma was pulling covers up and tucking them under her arm as she told us to get moving, and make it quick like the policeman told us. We were all climbing out of the back of our car, and Daddy was shuffling us pretty quickly into the back of a police car, while Momma threw the covers in on top of us. Seven of us all crowded in the back of that car, and a pile of blankets on top of us to boot.

Off we went like a rabbit, all of us hiding under the covers and whispering about going to jail. We were scared about what was happening, so we just stuck together and waited to see what would happen when we got to the jail.

It was a short ride, and just as quickly as we were loaded in the car, we were being pulled back out. Daddy was already inside when Momma walked us into the jail. Another policeman was standing there just inside and they were talking about what to do with us when we saw him point to a door across the room, "In there," he said, without even looking at us.

We were not putting up a fight and all walked to the door where Momma started pushing us inside. There I was, standing in a jail cell wondering why they would arrest a bunch of kids and a woman, we hadn't done anything wrong.

I was afraid looking through the bars at the front of the cell. I knew it was for bad people, criminals, ya know. Not a bunch of kids. The cell had bars on three sides and the back wall was made of concrete blocks. We could see right through to the cells on both sides and they could look right at us, too.

All of a sudden the door went closed and made a loud slamming noise and the whole room seemed to shake. All of us kids just sat on the mattress that was on the floor without saying a word. We were all holding on to each other with a pretty tight grip, we were afraid of being separated or something.

The policeman was still talking to Daddy, and we dare not say a word. Momma was shushing us kids to stay quiet, so she could listen.

Daddy finally walked into the cell and said, "We are staying here for the night". The police are not going to make us sleep out in the car, because the temperatures were going to be down to freezing overnight."

We were a little scared, but happy because it was warm in the jail with a big wood stove just outside the door. There were two more cells, one on each side of us, and there were men in both of them. I wondered if they were here because of the cold, or if they were the bad guys I should be afraid of.

After we settled down a bit, Daddy started talking to one of the men in the cell next to us. The man was tall and slender. His face was drawn and weathered with long whiskers that had not been taken care of for a long time.

I recognized his accent - he was from Tennessee. Daddy talked to him for a minute longer, and I could tell the old man was drunk as a hoot owl. He was making all kinds of noise and whooping it up with Daddy. It was just like the other men I had seen drunk on 'shine with Daddy.

All of a sudden they started laughing real loud. Daddy turned to Momma and said, "He wants to know what these kids did to get arrested," and Momma started laughing too. We started to relax a little and lay back on that mattress on the floor, it was warm as we listened to the fire crackle in the wood stove.

We were all glad to be in out of the cold, and I didn't care if it was a jail, it was warm and we all slept pretty well that night. I seemed to forget about being hungry for the minute, and just enjoyed a comfortable night of rest.

The next day we got a ride back out to the Hudson. Daddy had it fixed in no time, with the daylight to see and having the part he needed.

That was the first, and only time, I have ever been in jail. I was about 12 years old at the time, and to this day, I can close my eyes and see, smell, and hear it all over again. It's kind of funny, now.

Another time we were in Flagstaff, Arizona, in late June after working the onion planting in Texas. We were headed for cooler weather looking for work. It had been over 100 degrees every day for several weeks - it was unbearable.

As always, we were broken down on the side of the road several miles out of town. There was a small ranch house just a couple miles up ahead of us, and Daddy walked there to see if he could get us some help. We could see the farmhouse and barn from where we were. We also could see a big shade tree out front next to the road.

Daddy came back a bit later and said the old man had agreed to take him to town to see if he could get some parts for the old Hudson.

Several hours later Daddy was still gone, and it was getting hotter by the minute sitting on the side of that dusty road with other cars racing by us. The road stretched out in front of us as far as the eye could see.

There was nothing to see but hot dusty fields all around us, and no shade. But up around the house where Daddy had got help, there were trees. I could not take my eyes off the big one out by the road. It was an oasis in the desert to me. I could close my eyes and imagine what it would be like sitting under its shade with a cold drink in my hand, listening to the big ice chunks clanging against the side of the glass, and not a worry in the world.

I had a lot of opportunities to imagine things in my life being different, because we always had so little.

We sat on the road side for what seemed an eternity, with little water and little food. We were tired, hot and hungry by late that afternoon when Daddy came back. He jumped out of the old farmer's truck, thanked him and got right to work. He worked on the car for just a short time and told us all to get behind the car and to give him a push to see if it would start.

It started up, and we all jumped in hoping to cool off a bit as we rolled down the road, if even it was to be by the hot dry air.

Daddy said he wanted to stop and thank the fella again who helped him out, so we pulled up in front of the place on the side of the road under that great big shade tree. It was even bigger than it looked from down the road,once we got under it. It was huge, and it shaded what seemed like several acres around that house.

Oh, that tree was a welcome reprieve from the sun beating down on us all day - it felt like it was 50 degrees cooler under that big shade tree.

I asked Momma why we had to stay where we were on the side of the road all day instead of waiting under that shade tree. Momma said it was because it was not respectful and polite to just go on someone's property, even if all we were doing was looking for shade.

About that time, Daddy came back from the side of the house and started motioning his hand at us to get out of the car and come over to him. Mamma complained for a minute and started trying to fix her hair a bit and, all us kids started climbing out of that hot car and running for him, dirty faces and all.

Daddy took us around the back of the place and there sat this old man and his wife in some wooden chairs. They called out to us kids to come on over and have a seat on some benches next to them that were in a circle.

It was nice sitting under those shade trees as we pushed our bare feet into the cool grass, our toes and feet were so hot it felt like we were sticking them in the river.

The old lady got up, walked over to the back porch and retrieved a tray with a big pitcher of lemonade and a bunch of glasses on it. She immediately started filling some little glasses full of lemonade, and as she poured, I could hear the chunks of ice clanking on the side of the glass.

It was just like I had imagined many hours earlier.

I wanted to just grab that pitcher of lemonade and drink the whole thing right there. I could not wait to get a taste of that lemonade in my mouth.

We all started reaching for the glasses before she could even get them poured full. Mamma was slapping at our hands and told us, "Be polite, and wait until she hands you a glass." Momma kept saying, "Be careful, not to break the glasses." We were banging them around like the old Mason canning jars we were used to drinking from.

I drank that first glass so quick I'm not sure I even tasted it. It was so cold and I was so hot and thirsty. It was fantastic.

As I waited for another I stared at the cold pitcher sitting there with the water drops running down the sides. I rolled that chunk of ice around in my mouth and out over my dry lips, it was heaven.

The farmer's wife made sure each of us got another glass of that sweet lemonade, and that each of us got another small chunk of ice in the glass, too.

I have to say, that is the best lemonade I have ever tasted!

It was not long, and Daddy motioned for us to head for the car. We tipped those glasses up to our lips one more time just to make sure we had not left even a drop and then off we went. Momma and Daddy took a minute to thank those folks before they followed us back to the car. Back in that old car, we knew would be a long night of travel to try and make up some lost time.

Daddy said he had information that workers were needed in Bakersfield and Delano, for work in the cotton fields and the pay was good because it was early in the season.

We were headed for better work but a little hill stood between us and that work. It was called Tehachapi Pass.

We spent the night in Needles because we knew the Tehachapi Pass would take all day, and maybe more - as long as the car did not break down. The pass was about a four thousand foot climb, and it was very hot in Southern California.

We carried all the water we could because we knew the old car was going to be spitting it out as quick as we would pour it. There were barrels of water along the road about every mile or so for folks to use, because even the good cars would overheat on the Tehachapi Pass.

The steep climb would overheat the car engines and keeping water in them was all that kept us moving. There was always a line of folks at every barrel and sometimes it was difficult to get water, with folks keeping it for themselves.

We would usually try to cross early in the morning after the highway crews had filled the barrels for the day's use. Daddy said we were better off traveling in the early morning after a good night's sleep, because it is just as hot at night as it is in the early morning.

Our old car was loaded to the gills with kids and everything else we owned. I don't know how many miles that old car had on it, but I can tell you it didn't have many left. The only thing holding it together was baling wire and lots of prayers.

As it was, we had traversed that pass every year as we followed work from the south, up to the north through the Great San Joaquin Valley. I remember it would take a day or two, and there were several spots along the way where we could pull out and rest.

Most of those places were where everybody else was pulled over to let their car cool down and work on the ones that were broken down.

Every time I travel that pass now, I remember a different time and how difficult it was just to drive over that hill. I see places along the road where I know we were broken down, and at times seeing other cars stalled and overheated, and how I felt about it not being us, this time.

The highway crews still fill the water barrels along the roadside, and every time I cross the pass I see cars filling their overheated radiators from them. It seems as though not even the new cars can climb that pass without overheating.

Some things never change!

We were always chasing the next job and better pay. If we got there early in the season we could get a cabin, for us that was always a blessing.

The cabin meant we would not have to sleep out on the ground. I would rather sleep on the floor of a cabin then on the ground where bugs and critters would bother you while you were trying to sleep.

In the summer I was afraid to sleep out on the ground because roaches and snakes looked for warm places. A roach crawled into my ear one night, and Momma had a heck of a time getting it out.

You can't believe how bad it hurt having that roach in my ear; I thought I would die it hurt so bad. Momma poured Kerosene in it for hours, switching between pouring and looking, the whole time picking at it with Daddy's pocket knife and a splinter of wood.

One of the ladies working with us in the fields had some tweezers and Momma used them to finally pull that thing out. It hurt so badly and I remember crying the whole time. I never slept out on the ground like that again unless I had cotton or paper to stuff in my ears.

We generally used Route 66 in our travels back and forth through the west and east. It was the best highway at the time. All the fruit tramps used it as well, so usually there was plenty of help along the way.

Gas stations only would take cash or trade along Route 66. I think they knew we would wait around until late at night and steal the gas to keep going if they would not trade with us.

Most all the folks doing the same thing– it was how we survived. We could tell that a gas station was just ahead, because there would be a few cars along the roadside acting like they were working on their car until night so they could steal gas. Daddy would say something like, "Looky there, they're not even smart enough to have tools out on the ground by the car so it really will look like they are broken down." He knew the station owner would drive by and see them waiting and turn right back around to his station to protect it from theft, unless it looked like they were really broken down.

Daddy was pretty smart that way.

We could find hobo camps along the way into the towns where we stayed every year. We often stopped in the same places, and would see the same folks there every year, moving along Route 66 for the work, just like us.

A hobo camp or tramp camp, so called because hobos riding the trains would jump off in the camps just outside the train stops in town, so they would not be arrested by the railroad-yard police for illegally riding the train. The rail police were meaner than the town cops, and would beat you within an inch of your life for jumping the trains. That was justice in those days, and nobody could tell them not to, because the railroads had a lot of power and money. It was very dangerous to jump the trains and the hobos were a rough bunch of men.

Most of them were young men looking for work out West. We always had trouble with them drinking and coming around looking at us girls. I would keep away from all of them and would not even look when they called out to me. They were dirty, unshaven and had foul breath and filthy clothes - disgusting even for a fruit tramp.

My sister Alma was pretty loose with men and would bring them around. She would be out and on the hunt as soon as she could after we set up to stay a day or two.

She would wander around the camps, and she most often found older men to hang around with. Drinking was usually involved. It was not long before Daddy was popping some young guy in the nose to bring Alma back to our camp to try and save her honor. He did not know her honor had been lost long ago in a shed next to the cotton field we were working, just outside Bakersfield. Alma would say, "I left my flower back in Bakersfield any-way" when she would get back to our campsite. We dared not tell daddy what she meant, and so it went every time.

Daddy wasn't satisfied with just getting Alma back; he would beat those men pretty bad. I hope he didn't kill anybody. We never asked because Momma would tell us to shut up and be quiet about it, that it was, "Man business."

We all knew we would be leaving the next day, so Daddy could avoid being arrested by the local police, or risk having the man find him and work Daddy over with a group of his buddies.

Alma finally left for good with an older man; I think his name was Jim. I believe she was about 13 years old, at the time. Jim would have been 35, or so. This was pretty common at the time - young girls and older men.

We did see Alma and Jim in Tucson, the next year. She said they were married and happy. Daddy did not see it the same way and was fixin' to whip old Jim for taking off with Alma. She begged Daddy to leave Jim alone for taking off with her. He left it alone, and we went on our way.

It was less than a year later, and Alma was back with us because Jim was beating her all the time and she no longer was happy or healthy.

It was bad when she came back, because she started flirtin' with all the men, and it kept Daddy stirred up all the time. The rest of us kids hated it, but there was nothing we could do about it, we just had to suffer quietly if we knew what was good for us.

Several of my sisters did the same thing over the years. It was always the same when they left, too. They eventually would come back because the man they left with was beating them up, and foolin' around with other girls.

When my sister Donnie came back from running off, we got lucky; Donnie had become one Heck of a cook, and her biscuits were the best I ever ate.

She had run off with a man who already was married. He had two kids, and we had seen his wife and kids over the years at different camps, and we had worked with them in the same fields. Daddy was pretty upset because the guy's wife and kids had no way to move on or survive.

I guess he took off with Donnie while his wife and kids were out in the field one day. His wife looked all around for him that night because she and the kids did not even have a place to sleep. They had been sleeping in their car and when he took off with Donnie, the car went with him. All the blankets and everything they owned left as well.

We were in bad shape, too, and could not do anything about it, so we just moved on. I remember the look on that ladies face as we drove off that day, it was very sad, her sittin' there next to the field on a box with those kids and nothing else.

We next stopped for work in a little California town called Hughson. We decided to follow the Santa Fe Railroad tracks for work because there was always good work along the rail lines with most produce and fruit being shipped by rail.

We picked peaches, and it was good work. We were making good money for the time and were glad to be there.

After time, all of those little towns start to run together; they all looked the same to me. The work was hard in every one of them so it didn't matter what the name of the town was, it was just another town we worked through. That was all that seemed to matter to me as a very young child. As I got older I started to look those towns a bit different. I watched to see if it might be a good place to settle down with my own family in the future.

The funny thing is, I did return to live in Hughson after I got married and had kids of my own. It was as good a town as any, and there was work there in the fruit cannery. It had good schools and a library, too.

I wanted to go back to Hughson because I remembered there was a small grocery store there that was very good to us. When we first hit town, before Donnie ran off and we had to leave, the man who owned the store would let us get food, and pay for it when we found work and got paid.

I remember his last name as Gwinn. The grocery store was called, Save-More. It was on the main drag. I don't remember anything else about him except that he would sneak some little pieces of Andie to us kids. I thought that if that is how it is with people in this town, then that is where I want to

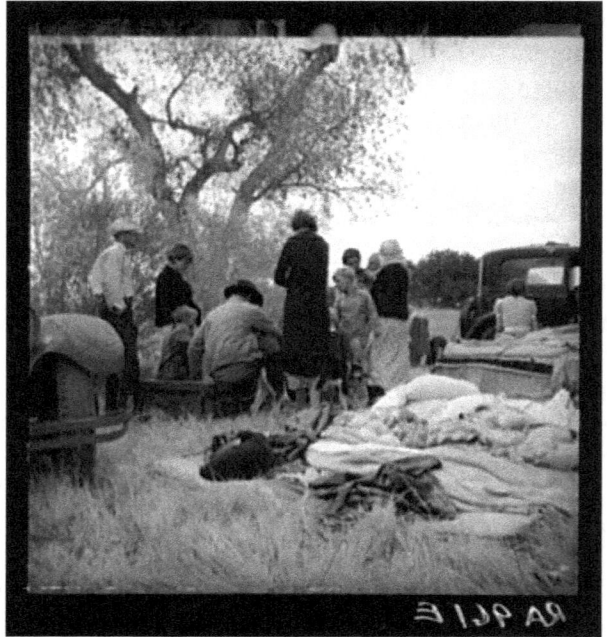

live.

Mr. Gwinn was awful good to us, and I guess he was to all the other families, too. He owned that store for a long time because he was still there when I moved back there as an adult some 10 years later. It still had the same name, too. I always shopped at that store, but never told him I was one of the kids he used to sneak candy too, maybe he knew already.

When you live like we did, it is easy to remember the people who were good to you. So many of the people looked down on us fruit tramps, and they did not want us in their town. We were good enough to pick their fruit and work in their fields, but not good enough to shop with them or go to school with their kids.

Funny how it was like that - it still is today for those who work in the fields. I always make sure I say hello to those folks when I see them in the grocery store. They are easy to spot, and the few things I see in the cart are for survival, just like when I was a kid in the same situation. Yeah; I sneak the kids a piece of candy if I can, and I try to find a little book or two their mom can read to them after a long day in the fields.

Some things never change; too bad, they need to!

CHAPTER SIX

A Pound And A Loaf

Route 66 - the Bologna Highway as we knew it - was a long and treacherous highway. Route 66 was a major highway that started near the Great Lakes and headed south through Texas and then west to the Pacific Ocean. It ran through the dust bowl of the south and mid-west, to the promised land of California.

Like so many other families before us we stopped at the local store for what we could afford and then kept moving.

The cars of that time were not fast like the cars of today. It was something to travel at forty- to forty-five miles-per-hour. Anything faster and the car would never last all the way to California. We looked like all the others: tired, hungry and dirty.

Food from a store was a bit of a treat for us. I can't tell you how many times I heard Daddy tell the man at the meat counter, "A pound and a loaf please."

We always had to get by on as little as possible. We could only buy a pound of bologna at a time. There was no way to store meat if we did not eat all of it, so he only bought enough for each of us to have a couple small pieces.

We had stopped at a small butcher shop on the edge of Tulsa, Oklahoma and Daddy asked for a pound of bologna and a loaf of bread. The man asked if he wanted it sliced as he pointed back to this shinny machine at the back of the counter.

He said it was a new machine that would slice it all up real nice and even. Of course this was all new to us and we told him as long as it was free he would try it.

First, the fella put the bread on it and started pushing and pulling the loaf of bread through it. Wow, I had never seen anything like that before. Slices all even and pretty, that should stop all the fighting about someone getting a thicker slice then the other.

Next, he put that big chunk of bologna up on it and asks, "How thick do you want each piece"?

Daddy paused for a minute as he was trying to figure out how to explain to him that he had ten people to feed with it and that he wanted it to make enough so each of us got a couple pieces. Well, in typical fashion, he looked right at the guy and told him, "Slice it so thin it's only got one side". The man laughed, made an adjustment on the machine, and he went to slicing.

They may not have had just one side but it was not far from it. As the slices came off I could see right through them they were so thin.

It is kind of funny as I look back with today's sliced and packaged lunch meat.

Back in those days there was no such thing as bread already sliced and in a package, same goes for sandwich meat. Everything had to be done by the butcher, or you had to do it yourself.

You can't imagine how many fights we had as kids over how things were sliced up. When it was meat, we would all watch pretty close when Momma sliced things for us to make sure we got the same as the next.

Most of the time, we had more avocado, onion or tomato on the sandwich than anything else because we were allowed to glean some from the fields we were working in.

We never had to worry about a big thick slice of whatever we were picking, even if they were green. It was hard because our meals were all the same thing – breakfast, lunch and dinner –and you better not do any complaining about what we were eating unless you wanted a slap across the face. Things were different in those days, and a good slap in the face was pretty common, it was how parents kept their kids in line.

Maybe it wouldn't hurt to have a bit of that today. Not abuse, respect.

It was too much to ask for something to drink except water, which was free.

Every now and then we would get to share a soda pop. Some of the stations and stores had pop for sale and, while Daddy kept the man busy, we would try to steal one or two.

The signs on the door usually said, "No Fruit Tramps or Vagrants Allowed inside," because they knew we would steal if we had a chance. Most of the time Daddy or Momma were the only ones allowed inside while the rest of us waited outside. If the storekeeper did not have someone to help

him watch all of us, we would get what we could. There was no way Daddy was going to buy us anything like soda, so Curtis would try to get it while we kept the others busy watching us, we would act like we were trying to steal something else and keep their attention. The soda machine always was next to the door or out on the front of the store, so it made it pretty easy to get one or two.

After we took off, we would take it out and ask Daddy or Momma to open

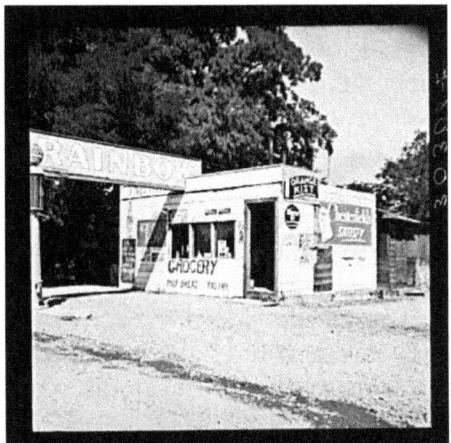

it. Every now and then Daddy would gripe about us taking it but Momma or Little Granny would tell him to let us have it and that was usually the end of it. We knew we could not afford to buy it and since we already had it he was not going to turn around and take it back; besides that, he knew it was not worth the fight he would get from Momma and Little Granny.

It was survival most of the time that drove us to steal - all except for the pop, and we just liked it - it was a real treat. Stolen or not, it tasted so sweet and good.

I know Curtis would take other things for us; Curtis would help put in the gas by telling the fella he knew how to do it and ask if he could try. Then he would put in a little extra, and then act like he did not know what he had done. We drove a lot of extra miles on that stolen gas. Daddy would just tell the station attendant that he did not have the money to cover it, and argue about the fella wanting to siphon it back out. Daddy never let anyone take back what we rightfully stole. Gas was eleven cents a gallon, and we needed every penny we had for food.

Some of the stations raised the price of gas for all of us headed for the fields in the South and West, so we didn't have too much sympathy for them when we beat them out of a little fuel.

Every once in a while the attendant would make Daddy help him out with something else to pay for the extra gas. It seemed like we always ended up with more stuff when he was done then the gas was worth. Daddy was a pretty good horse trader and talker, so he would help out to pay for the extra and end up with another tire, a battery or parts of some kind. Not to mention what we got when the fella was not looking. Pretty quick he would give up trying to keep up with all of us, and knowing he was losing more than he was making, he would send us on our way.

Momma sometimes would just laugh because she knew that if Curtis was made to stay around for awhile, it would cost you - he would take things even if he didn't know what they were.

If we couldn't use them on our car, we would sell or trade for other things we could use.

As I look back, it is a little hard to believe I used to live that way. At the time, it did not seem to matter too much about all the other people and whatever problems they had, I wanted to survive. Daddy told us we had to survive the best way we knew how, and that meant we did whatever we had to do.

I don't want to make us sound like a bunch of thieves who were stealing things because we were too lazy to work, we were not lazy; we were desperate.

The Depression did a lot of things to people and made them do things they never would have before the Depression. People were honest and hard working and helped each other out; the Depression took all that away from us.

It may be hard for others to understand if they did not go through this, too. Desperation causes you to think differently, hunger is pretty powerful. Not just a little hungry, like when you can go somewhere and know food is there, but a gnawing pain in your gut that keeps you awake at night. There weren't the organizations of today that provide food for the field workers and their families.

This kind of hungry will make you do bad things because you have nowhere to go for food, and it has been some time since you last ate. It is the kinds of hungry that will not let you just walk away from a place where you see food. Your mind starts to work on you and make you believe that is the only food left in the world today and if you do not take it, you will starve another day.

A person only can take so much of that kind of mental and physical torture before you do what you have to for that food. I never killed anyone for food, but I probably thought about it in terms of robbing a store where there would be enough food for all of us for a long time. It almost seemed worth it in my mind.

Hunger is a powerful emotion and it will make you a different person. Do not judge me or others who had to do this, unless you are willing to suffer the same hunger pain and desperation first. You will eat anything, and I do mean anything that looks or smells good enough to satisfy your hunger.

I can't say for sure, but I think we ate horse meat at a camp in Kern County sometime around Christmas of 1943. As always, times were hard and with the war going on everything was in short supply, work and especially food. Everything was going to the war effort.

One of the families in the camp had been pulling logs out of the hills down to the camps where Daddy would cut it for firewood for all the families staying there.

The Ranch Forman sold much of it in town, and like many of the other men, my Daddy helped cut and load wood every day through the winter for work while there was no farming work to be done. We were one of the lucky ones to have even that work during the winter.

That family had a horse he had used all the time. It was always around the camp somewhere, and some of us kids would chase it with sticks and throw rocks at it for something to do.

Several of the men in camp had killed something just before Christmas over by the big grove of eucalyptus trees

50

and were butchering it. A bunch of us kids from the camp went over to watch, the men there ran us off and told us to go back home.

I looked for Daddy but did not see him, and when we got back to the cabin we told Momma what happened over at the grove. We asked if Daddy was over there with the other men and Momma said he was. She said the wood cutter had asked him to come and help him butcher some meat for the winter. She said he had left early that morning before we got up, and she did not expect to see him until late that evening.

Several hours later, after dark, Daddy came home. He smelled pretty bad, like blood. He washed up and told us kids to come help carry some meat into the cabin to hang up. We carried several big chunks in off the back of Daddy's car, and he hung them from the ceiling beams. I had never seen so much meat at one time.

Daddy told us it was a pig and said the ranch gave it to all of us for Christmas. We had no reason to think differently. Every time Momma cooked it, we ate every bit. It was nice to have plenty of meat, and we ate some most every meal.

As I think back though, I am pretty sure it was that old horse we chased around. I can't recall seeing that horse after that day and just figured the wood cutter just left it up where he was cutting wood or that it had died or was stolen.

At the time, we didn't know any different and I am not sure it would have mattered anyway, we were hungry and it tasted just fine to us.

I laugh as I think about that old saying now; you should never look a gift horse in the mouth - or the eyes either, for that matter - because you may have to eat one someday.

I wish it was different, but that meat was a big deal to us. We did not get to eat meat that often and it really helped in the winter, especially for Christmas.

I am thankful those men ran all us kids off so we did not have to see it. I don't know how it would have affected me as a kid to know what it was.

God protects kids from things like that, I think, and he took care of us on that day.

It was a very difficult time and all of us were looking for a blessing of some kind, especially when it had to do with food and comfort. Many never recognize a blessing because they do not know what to look for, and even if they did find it, they would not have known what to do with it. As a kid I did not know or understand all the complications of being an adult or a parent with hungry kids to provide for. Now I do understand, and I'm grateful that I recognize all I have and have been given. I do not forget those who are still suffering and in need, I pray they will find blessings and be thankful for them when they receive them.

We were just grateful for the meat at that moment - it would not matter a day later, as that day would bring its own challenges.

We spent the winter there and Daddy worked most of it in that area for several farms and delivering wood to the folks in town. It was a pretty good winter in comparison to many others - we had a cabin, Daddy had work and we had food. The old cabin had a wood stove and the outside had been covered with scrap wood to keep the wind out.

I was pretty lucky because I had an old shirt filled with cotton seed for a pillow. The foreman at a camp in Bakersfield gave it to me the day when we took our sacks in for the end of the cotton harvest.

I had been working every day in the field because I knew we would be leaving soon and would need the extra money for the road. All the kids were in the field every day - I was not very old, but could pick like most men. The man at the Gin would talk to me every day when we would turn in our picking slips. The foreman kind of liked me because I always worked so hard as a kid.

I think he knew we were leaving, and on the last day we went up to the Gin, he gave me this shirt, tied like a small bag. It was nice and soft. He gave it to me and said I could use it as a pillar. I just smiled, and thanked him for it.

I asked Daddy what a pillar was and he told me I could put my head on it when I went to sleep. We laughed about him calling it a pillar because Daddy and Momma had always called the rolled up cloths we used bumps.

Daddy told me that foreman must have gone to the Gin shed and scooped up the seed from under the thresher where the cotton is separated from the seed. There is always a big pile of it there where it falls out of the cracks of the machine. He also said that the farm would keep all that seed and sell it for stuffing in pillows and bed mattresses for the rich.

Well, anyway the pillar was very nice and it was so soft. The other kids would fight with me to use it. Sometimes they would try to go to bed early and take it, so I would have to use my bump instead. Momma would take it from them and give it back to me.

It was something to fight over, and as it was, we did not need much of an excuse to fight.

Sometimes Little Granny would use it during the day if she took a nap. I did not mind. She said it was the best bump she ever had.

One day after her nap, Little Granny was sitting on the step into the cabin when we came in from the field. She had a big mark on the side of her face. Momma started asking all kinds of questions about what had happened to her and telling Granny she wanted to know who did it to her.

Little Granny was getting mad at Momma and both of them were raising their voices at each other. Daddy started laughing at them and pointing at Granny's face. The more Daddy laughed, the madder Momma got. She was all red in the face and swinging her finger around pointing at Granny and then to other cabins nearby asking if they were the ones who did it.

We kids did not know what was going on, and were a little scared because everybody was yelling and pointing fingers. We knew Daddy would be fighting someone pretty soon, and we would have to move again at night.

Daddy kept pointing at Grannies face, and then he told Momma it was Betty Girl's dammed old pillar that did it. He kept laughing and just saying, "That pillar did it and boy did it do it up right."

The pillar had made a big spot on Granny's face, right under her eye. It looked like Granny had a black eye, and she did not even know it. Momma thought someone had hit Granny and that she wasn't telling who it was.

Granny started rubbing under her eyes and smeared it all over her face. It was so funny. We were all laughing, and Momma was so mad because she was embarrassed about thinking someone had hurt Little Granny.

Granny's face stayed that way for a couple days. I won't say what we started calling her, but we had fun with it. Granny did not seem to care as long as it was only us kids that were saying it. She did not want to hear it from Daddy and she made that pretty clear the first time he said it to her.

The pillar stayed with me for several years until bugs got in it and Daddy made me throw it away. By then, the seeds were breaking up inside the bag and it was kind of a mess. It would leave brown spots on my face in the morning after sleeping on it all night. It also started to smell a bit, and Momma said there was no way to wash seeds. Finally, I scattered the seeds on the ground next to the water ditch we were camping by.

I had hoped it would grow something, and I would be able to see it someday if we worked back to that field again. I did not know if it would grow, and I guess it did not really matter. I missed that pillar and thought about that old man that gave it to me for several years after.

I don't remember his face, but I do remember his scratchy voice, it was not like any other voice I had ever heard before. Momma later told me he had some kind of problem with his voice, like cancer or something, and that is why he sounded like he did.

He was nice to me and that pillar was a nice memory. I felt special because if it. I had something the other kids did not have. It was something they wanted, but it was mine, and I did not have to share it if I did not want to. Sometimes I would share it with Midge and we would whisper ourselves to sleep about having it as our own. It is still a special memory for me and I think of it every night when I put my head on my pillow.

Granny was mad at Daddy for all the teasing he did about that pillar over the years and miles as we traveled. She threatened to poison his food and get rid of him if he said another word about it. I don't think Granny would have done any such thing, but she let us believe she would. We would tell Daddy he better mind his Ps and Qs or we would get Granny to poison him.

I miss little Granny, she was special. She made sure that the kids had a safe place and food, when she could do anything about it. I think Granny would look for food and or even beg for it, if she needed to, so she could help look out for us.

I do remember sometimes eating, but Granny, Momma and Daddy would not eat anything. Granny used to tell us they had already eaten, or that they were not hungry. I think we knew better as kids, but were not sure what to do about it. We would just eat and be glad for it.

I don't remember ever being told not to eat all we had at a meal; we never left anything in the pan. I don't know how many times the adults went hungry so the kids could eat and not have to go to bed with empty bellies.

Daddy and Granny would put a big pinch of snuff in their mouth and sit back while we ate. Momma would make sure we had all shared equally what we had. She sometimes would give me an extra spoonful because I had to work every day in the fields with Daddy, and the other kids usually would make an excuse to get out of working, so my reward for a day's work was one extra scoop. I was glad to have it too.

I could not and would not make up excuses not to work; I had to be tough and did not want to be thought of as lazy, if not for Daddy then for myself. I guess I wanted to be strong and not let others think they could do more than me at anything. I had to be a champion at everything. That was expected of me.

If you were lazy you also were weak. I never wanted to be seen as weak, not even by my own family. I know Daddy admired that about me and he would sometimes say things about how tough I was. It was usually when he was calling one of the other kids lazy- I think that made the others resentful of me.

I believed from a very young age that I would have to work hard and be stronger than anybody else to make it for myself. Toughness was a characteristic that was admirable in people and it was what Momma had looked for in a man when she was young, so I thought that was what I needed to be so someone would want me.

There was not a lot of talk about being a lady or being educated; for me it was work hard and be tough. These were the necessary qualities for a good husband or wife. Momma said everything will come natural; there is nothing we would need to learn or practice for a man. She said men were pretty simple creatures. They only have a few things on their minds, and you will learn what that is soon enough.

She said as long as we learned to work hard and cook we had two out of three. I later learned what the third was – and, it came natural just like Momma said.

It was tough to learn the lessons in those days. We had little, but were still able to laugh and have fun. All of us kids would fight no matter what the issue; we would make something up if we needed to just to fight about it. It gave us something to do as we traveled all those miles over all those dusty rough roads of America.

It was the same when I started raising my own kids. I sometimes would laugh at how it sounded - just like when I was a kid fighting with my brother and sisters.

The lessons were tough for all of us and still are today for young families who are fighting to survive. There are more programs available for families today than there were then, education is mandatory, and kids can get medical help, too.

There are so many organizations that will give out food, good food to families who are in need. I wish we would have had that in my childhood.

Programs are better today because of what we went through back in those days. It would be nice to be recognized by someone for the sacrifice we endured as kids, and how we fought for better conditions as we grew older.

Many of us became very active in the fight to improve conditions for farm workers and the poor as we started to raise our own families. We did this in hopes that if they had to work in the fields; it would not have to be the same as it was for me.

Poor blacks and whites did most of that kind of work back then and forced most of the change for what it is today. We have been lost in the fabric of other cultures who claim it has only been their fight and, they are the only ones who have ever been required to work in the harsh conditions of farm labor.

I am not against anyone who suffers these conditions, but I want people to know that we paved the way for the changes, and would like that story to be told as well.

For this reason, I am grateful for the suffering so I can try to make it better for the coming generations who must do this kind of work.

We do not want to be forgotten in history. Remember, Respect, Be grateful.

CHAPTER SEVEN

My First Camp

There are a couple of camps that I remember as places I would look forward to going to each year. We would return to some of the camps on a yearly basis - several of the farms would give us the best cabins if we would return every year to help them with their harvest. Jobs were hard to find, but so was good experienced help.

One camp was in Hughson, California. It was the camp that had the best cabins and paid really well for those days.

I also liked it because I could get a job at the loading docks and not have to work in the fields. All the farmers brought the fruit to be sorted, dried or shipped to the loading docks.

The crop in Hughson was peaches - they were the best in the world. They were sweet and delicious, and the juice would run down your chin as you ate them.

You ask what this has to do with camps. Food! I have a hazy recollection of those camps all over the country, however most of them were the same: dirty and hot or freezing and lonely.

It is hard to distinguish one cabin full of holes and filth- because of the lack of care for those who had to live in them - from another. Animals got better treatment and had better buildings to live in than we sometimes did.

When we were in a good cabin, it was kind of special for us. A good cabin had more than one room, so we did not all have to sleep in the same room all the time. The better ones had running water inside, and the best ones - in Hughson - had a real indoor toilet. It was the only cabin I remember as a child that had an indoor toilet. It actually was fun to have to go to the bathroom and get to use the toilet, and then be able to flush it. Wow! Indoor plumbing was rare in the type of camps we could afford.

The cabin in Hughson also was close to work and that was a very convent bonus.

The loading docks were just across the street. I could walk to the docks for my work – which I really appreciated. Momma and I both got jobs at the dock helping to sort peaches coming in from the fields. We both got to work together, and when the sorting was slow, we worked cutting peaches for dehydration - my job was to lay them out on the trays for drying in the sun.

We did peaches most of the time, but sometimes we sorted and dried apricots. When we worked picking all the time, I used to wonder where all that fruit went. After working on the dock, I knew what they did with all that luscious fruit. I'm glad I had that experience.

Daddy worked for the same ranch every year, and that man treated him pretty good. He offered Daddy different jobs every year- driving equipment or checking the others pickers work for bruised fruit –but Daddy always would pick fruit, because that's where he could make the most money.

The foreman always gave Daddy the best rows to pick, and helped him by keeping plenty of lug boxes on hand so he did not have to go look for them himself, and fall behind. Even with only the one hand, he could pick as fast as the others could pick with two hands.

Daddy would ride from our cabin in town, out to the ranch with a couple of other men. He liked this because he did not want to drive his old car all the time, and it saved us money.

Daddy did all he could for the family, and tried to make sure he gave us every chance to "make it" wherever we were. Hughson was very good to us and very good for Midge.

There was a Doctor in that town that looked after Midge for free. I think his name was Dr. Bigelow, and he had a habit of coming through the camp to help those who needed medical care. He was very kind and Midge really liked him, too.

See, there were many things that made a good camp for fruit tramps, the town was good to us and did not treat us like outsiders, the Doctor would help all of us, and the cabin itself was one of the best ever. The grocery store was helpful and nice too.

We always would look ahead in the season to see how long it would be before we would be there again, and of course, argue about who was going to sleep in which room in the cabin .It was something to fight about and keep us busy until we could get to Hughson.

Many of the same families would be there every year, and usually the same problems with the same kids. We would plan how we were going to handle this kid or that kid because of what had happened the year before.

Some of the fights were like the Hatfield and McCoy's of old times. Of course, it did not take long for the fights to start once we were there, it seemed like it was meant to be.

We would fight with the Barker kids every year. It did not matter what the issue was, just that we would look for them as soon as we got there, and then start in. We had some pretty bad fights over the years, and the older we got the worse the fights were. All of the kids would be fighting, and then pretty soon Daddy and Momma joined in, too. Not just kid fighting but fist fighting. We would tear at their clothes and try to bloody them up if we could, that is how we declared the winner.

I don't know what happened to that family after we stopped going to the Hughson camp, but I bet they found someone else to fight, just like we did.

The last time I remember seeing them, they had a nice car, and boy was it shiny. All the families were admiring it, and wondering what bank they had robbed to get to get such a fine ride.

I don't remember what kind of car it was, but we were not having any of it because they were arch rivals. We threw some rocks at it, and Curtis broke out one of the side windows.

There were about ten of us from the camp that were all throwing the rocks, so no one could prove that it was Curtis who had thrown the one that broke the window. I know it was him because I saw him run up by it and chuck that big rock right at the window. When it broke, we all went to running. They came out of their cabin chasing us, but there were too many of us and we scattered all directions like a bunch of Quail.

They recognized us, of course, and were yelling our names as we ran off to hide.

Later, when the police showed up at our cabin we all denied we did anything, or were even there. The police could not do anything because they could not prove it was Curtis who broke the window, and that was our last year there so we always felt like we won since they could not get us back.

We had an old car at the time, and Daddy joked that even if they came and threw rocks at our car, we would not know because it already had so many dents in it, he would not be able to pick out new ones from the old ones. He said they might do him a favor and knock some of the old dents out of it because he was tired of looking at the old ones.

We bought that car in Fallon, Nevada from a man who was working on a sheep ranch. Daddy got it cheep, and he swore it was a better car then the one he traded to that old man. It's true that it had fewer holes in the bottom but it was so dented up on every side it looked like we had been in a wreck. Daddy said the old man used it to help herd sheep and cattle, and all the dents were from the animals running in to it.

Daddy got drunk with the old guy, traded cars and off we went. Momma said he," got took" on the deal, but Daddy wasn't having any of it because he didn't have to work on it much alongside the road. That was always a win for all of us.

We traded that car a few months later for another one before we left Hughson. The man we traded with was headed off for the war. He was dressed in his uniform, and looked like he was pretty serious business when he came to our cabin.

I remember his name - it was Creekmore. He wanted to sell the car because he was headed to an army post in Colorado, and then off to somewhere in the South Pacific, as he told it.

Creekmore told us he was from a town up north in Washington State called Lake Chelan, where he was an apple farmer. He said they were the best apples in the world and a lot of money was to be made picking them. He and Daddy talked a lot about farming and sort of became friends. Momma called him Daddy's drinking buddy. He was in Hughson visiting his girlfriend before he left for the war.

Momma did not like Creekmore because he had a good looking girlfriend he always brought around with him and that was a problem for Momma. She and Daddy had already had a fight over it. She was afraid Daddy would spend too much time looking at Creekmore's girlfriend and not pay attention to what he was doing with buying the car. She said she figured Creekmore knew exactly what he was doing, and she was sure it would cost us.

Daddy said he was going to get old Creekmore' shined up -"drunk on liquor," and take advantage because the soldier didn't have much time before he had to leave. Daddy could drink pretty heavy.

Daddy waited until Creekmore was just a couple days from leaving, and then started talking about buying the car. It was a nice blue Plymouth and it had lots of room. We were all hoping Daddy would buy it because it would be the nicest car we ever owned. We had made good money that year in Hughson, and we would soon be leaving for New Mexico to cut wood all winter.

The long drive would be nice in that car, and not being broke down all the way there would be nice too. Daddy always got pretty grumpy when we were broke down and would do a lot of yelling at all of us - like we could have done something about it.

Daddy and his friends got 'shined up for two days straight with ol'Creekmore. Momma said it was going to be bad one way or the other because of all the drinking. We tried to stay out of sight of them and the other men who were drinking with him.

Daddy said he and Creekmore were old horse traders and would work out some kind of deal. Well they did, I guess, because when we left town we drove off in that blue Plymouth.

Good thing the Barkers never saw that car, or we probably would have left with some dents and fewer windows, just like they did.

Momma griped at Daddy for a thousand miles about that car and kept saying, "You lost your shirt to ol'Creekmore, big horse trader!" She was pretty mad.

All of us kids wondered why that man would take Daddy's shirt, they weren't much good. We kept watching to see if Daddy had all his shirts. We learned later what Momma was talking about and had a good laugh about what we thought Momma meant.

That was the best car we ever owned, and it was real nice to have the extra room in the back because all us kids were getting bigger by then.

Daddy did the same with this car as he did with all the others - he took out the back seat and sold it for whatever he could get.

The seat took up too much room, and we couldn't get all our stuff in the car if we left the seat in. We had to pile all our possessions in the back, and then fit all of us kids in too. Momma, Daddy and Little Granny sat in the front seat.

Midge could not bend her legs very well, so she had to have room to stick them straight out because of the polio and her leg braces.

So ended another season, and the memories, at Hughson.

Hughson marked the end of summer for us, and we knew we would be heading for a place to spend most, or all, of the winter. It would be sometime in late September or early October when we would drive out.

This particular year we were headed for Ruidoso, New Mexico. Daddy had an offer to cut wood there for the winter, as he had done for the past several years.

The wood was cut from of the Lincoln National Forest. The logs were dragged down out of the hills and to a rail yard where they were loaded on trains headed for the East Coast. I don't remember what they were doing with it there - firewood I think – but, it was good money for us, and it meant none us kids would not have to work much. With all of the US coal production going to the war effort, folks needed firewood to heat their homes and businesses. This was good for us, and we were glad to have the winter work.

The camp in Ruidoso was nice, like the Hughson camp. The cabins were nice in comparison to others provided for farm workers. These had a wood stove in the corner of the room - and because Daddy was cutting wood - we always had plenty to burn keeping that cabin nice and toasty all winter.

We were excited to be headed for Ruidoso. The car was the best we had ever had to drive, but as it was for us, there always was something that had to happen to make our trip - let's say - exciting.

We had traveled all day and well into the night through California, headed to New Mexico. Daddy said we would stop somewhere and spend the night before we got to White Sands, New Mexico.

Daddy said he did not want to be out on the ground during October in White Sands. We didn't know what his problem was with it, and we didn't care. We just wanted to stop and get out of the car because we were awful tired from all the hours packed in the back of that car.

Daddy would not stop for anything, and when he did stop it was get what we needed and get moving again, like we were in some kind of race. He knew other men would be on their way to the logging camp too, he wanted to get there early so he could get us a good cabin at the bottom of the hill. He knew the big wood pile for the hired hands was at the bottom of the hill, and we would not have to carry wood for the cabin as far. That would make Momma happy, us kids too because we were the ones who had to fetch it every day.

We stayed on the road as long as we could - but Momma was griping, Midge was crying and all us kids were squirming. When Daddy finally couldn't take it anymore, he did exactly what he didn't want to and pulled over next to a big rock bluff just outside White Sands.

The rocks stood tall above the road and made for good cover from the wind that always seemed to blow there at night. It was a small canyon and the traffic was pretty light, so we did not move far off the roadway to set up our camp.

Daddy kept gripping about having to stop there, but Momma insisted. All the kids were happy to get out of the car. We spent several hours playing on the rocks and climbing up the hillside while Momma and Little Granny cooked something to eat.

Daddy did not seem to mind resting, he fell asleep as soon as he sat out a tarp and a blanket on the ground next to the car - he called it a "pallet."

When Momma started calling for us to come back for dinner, we started making our way back to the camp from all over that hillside where we were playing and exploring. Then Daddy woke up. He got pretty mad because we were climbing around the hillside and didn't stay right by the car like he told us too. He was yelling for us to get back to the car and scolded each of us as we got back for dinner.

That was the end of playing in the rocks and on the hills, because Daddy made us stay right by him the rest of the evening. He said we were in country that was known for all kinds of bad stuff like tarantulas, snakes and scorpions.

We were just kids and wanted to play, but we knew he usually was right about those kinds of things. He had been living out on the road most of his life. We did what Daddy told us to and spent the rest of the evening pretty close to the camp and practiced our rock throwing. Curtis did not need much practice, but the rest of us did.

We kids finally ran out of gas sometime late in the evening, Momma and Little Granny made up our pallet for the night. It consisted of the big tarp we used for a tent and other times we put our blankets out on it so we weren't on the damp ground. Because we only were staying for the night, Momma laid the tarp out and we laid our blankets on one half of it and then she folded the rest of it up on top of us, in case it rained in the night.

We had fun doing it that way and did not mind being under the tarp and out on the ground. My blankets were warm and all of us went to sleep pretty quickly, as I remember it.

Suddenly, we were all awaken by Daddy's yelling, "Myrtle, get the kids up, hurry, hurry!" He was scaring us because he just kept yelling to get us all in the car - I had never heard Daddy yell like that before. He was scared and his voice was loud and kind of broken.

Momma was hurrying us up off the ground and over to the car. We were still half asleep trying to all climb into the back of the car at the same time – pushing every which way and knocking each other down as we hurried at Daddy's insistence to get in quickly.

He never stopped yelling to hurry and we started crying - scared at all the commotion of being woken up and having to hurry into the back of the car. Daddy was afraid - and that scared us.

We finally all were in the car and Daddy was telling us to quiet down and keep the windows up. We had no idea what was wrong, but we knew Daddy did not get scared about much so this must be bad. All of us were looking out the windows for what scared him and why he was yelling in the middle of the night scaring us half to death in the process. I remember looking at the other kids with their faces pressed against the car windows for some sign of the problem.

We did all quiet down, I could hear noises coming from outside, noises like I had never heard before, and it was getting closer. The noise became louder and louder as we all watched out into the darkness, afraid for what we might see. The canyon rock walls were so tall above us that the moonlight was barely evident.

We listed for a few more minutes and, by this time, it was really loud and we knew whatever it was, was right outside the car. I heard Little Granny whisper something to Daddy and he said, "Yep," in a loud voice, "just what I thought, and why I sure as heck didn't want to stop here. I knew we were too close to time for those dang things to migrate through here. It looks like we will have to wait for morning before we can go back outside; I think they only move at night."

All of us started asking what it was - the sound was kind of a scraping noise -it's hard to explain. It was like crickets scraping on a chalk board or something, but it was loud and all around us. It was overwhelming, and I was so afraid. I wondered what kind of monsters were surrounding us and what would they do with us?

Daddy got the small kerosene lantern lit and slowly opened his car window holding the lantern out lighting up the ground. The ground where we just had been sleeping was completely covered with big, brown, furry tarantulas. There were so many we couldn't even see the tarp or the blankets we had just been sleeping on. They were a wave of motion as they all crawled along together.

Daddy said in a broken loud voice, "Tarantulas, dirty stinking tarantulas. I hate those dang things." He pulled the lantern back into the car, quickly closing the window to keep them from getting in.

We started to cry again because we now thought we would be carried off by the mass of tarantulas and be killed and eaten.

I had seen a couple of tarantulas before but that was as we drove by them on the road. Every time we would see one, Daddy would cuss at them like they owed him money or something. I did not know Daddy was so afraid of them.

Little Granny talked to us and helped to calm us down explaining that it was breeding migration and all the male tarantulas were out looking for a girlfriend, not us, and that we were not food to them. It took a little while before we decided we were safe in the car and the tarantulas did not care about us.

I was sure grateful about that new car; it did not have holes in the bottom like all our other cars in the past, so none of those things could climb in after us. I can tell you though, we did some pretty close inspections of the floor and everywhere else we thought one of them might try to climb in while we waited for morning.

It took several hours for them critters to move on through, and I could tell Daddy hated the entire time just like us kids. He would not even look out the window and just kept gripping about Momma convincing him to stop there.

He said he had heard stories about the tarantulas in that part of the country and warned Momma that it was close to the time of year when they start to migrate and he did not want to take a chance of having to see so many of them. Daddy settled down after they passed but still made all of us stay in the car until morning and it was light enough to see.

I can report that not one got in, and we were not carried off and eaten by tarantulas.

Little Granny got tired of waiting and out she went, telling us kids to wait in the car until she had a chance to shake out the tarp and blankets making sure none of those critters stayed behind. Little Granny gave everything a good look as she would shake them out. She was piling up the tarp and blankets on the top of the car when Daddy started telling her to be careful and not scratch up the paint on his new car.

Little Granny paused for just a second before she told Daddy, "Well then, come on out and help me shake 'em all out, Homer. You can hold them so I don't have to put 'em up on the car. You're not scared are ya, Homer?"

Little Granny was about the only person on the planet who could get away with talking that way to him. Little Granny knew he would not dare cross her; I loved Little Granny for that.

Well, as you might imagine, he didn't stop complaining the whole time but he stayed in the car and waited like Momma and all us kids for the go ahead from Granny that the tarantulas all had gone on their way. I guess he was more afraid of tarantulas then he was worried about scratches on that car he paid too much for - "the ol' horse trader."

We packed up the camp and got back out on the road for the short trip on into Ruidoso. We would call it home for that winter, and as luck would have it, the early trip there paid off with us getting one of the better cabins at that camp at the bottom of the hill.

The indoor plumbing worked most of the winter - with the exception of the dozen or so times it would freeze and Daddy would have to build a fire and fan the heat up under that old cabin to thaw out the pipe. We really didn't mind though because it was so much better than others we had lived in over the season. It sure beat sleeping out on the ground and worrying about being carried off by tarantulas.

The first week we were there it rained every day and the thunder and lightning was pretty impressive, too. The thunder would shake the cabin all the way down to the wood foundation.

The cabin had one hole in the roof, and Daddy was able to fix it with some scrap roofing material from the camp foreman. It was unusual for cabins to be in such good shape, as they already had been standing for 25 years by this time. The foreman lived just up the road, and I think he watched over them real close and kept them in good condition for the help.

Because it was a logging camp, wood was easy to come by. Many of the loggers had some skills with carpentry, and made sure each cabin was up to snuff for the winter crew.

Because of the Depression, and so many men looking for work, the foreman could be picky about who worked for him, especially through the winter when many of the families who were content in the Hobo camps during the warm seasons, started looking for something with walls and a wood stove to stay warm through the winter.

This man respected Daddy and made sure he had a place. Daddy respected him and he worked very hard for this job. The days were long and sometimes the snow was deep but work went on no matter the conditions. Daddy worked like a team of mules up in those hills - cutting and rolling timber down to the pull trail to be dragged to the rail yard.

Pull trails were really no more than a rut in the ground so the logs would not roll off down the mountain taking the pull-horses down to their deaths. However, by the end of winter, the ruts were pretty deep after having hundreds of logs dragged through them. We would play in them and the "skidders" would yell at us as we would wait until the last minute to jump clear of the team of horses pulling the logs.

Although firewood was a big part of wintertime work because most of the coal production was being used by the war effort, this year would be a bit different. Daddy's foreman at the logging camp was just a young kid. Many of the older men had gone off to the war and the younger men had to take up the farms and businesses of their families while dad and/or the older brothers were away in battle. This "young kid," as Daddy called him, was the son of the man who owned the camp and logging operation.

The kid's dad had left him in charge of things, and he was in kind of a bad spot - the he did not know much about the operation he and was not prepared to deal with a bunch of savvy loggers, daddy said.

Daddy tried to help look after the kid because he had worked for the owner of the logging company for many years and had been treated well.

He felt like he owed it to the fella, because he had gone off to the war and he knew many of the other men would take advantage of the kid, causing the family to lose the company.

There's always been a struggle between survival and loyalty - which are hard to observe equally - and that struggle hasn't changed, has it?

Trouble was no stranger in the camps and could strike even the most well-meaning people. Daddy's trials came in trying to help the young man. Some of the other men in camp got mad because he would keep them from taking advantage of the kid. They would tell him it was none of his business, and that usually did not bode well with a man like my Daddy who had a short temper and the heart to back it up.

Daddy fought for that kid all season and helped him to make it through that first year he was in charge. The kid asked him lots of questions almost every morning just outside our cabin door, and we would listen to Daddy tell him what was going on and how to watch for cheating.

Some of the horse-team drivers would get their log counted, drag it down the pull trail just a short distance and then,loop around, unhook the team and pull the same log from the other end to make it look like a new log out of the hills. They'd take that log through for a second count by one of their buddies marking the log tally. They would get paid twice for pulling the same log, and Daddy knew this old trick from many years of logging. Daddy told the kid to watch for how the dirt and snow would be stuck to the front end of the log. If dirt and snow was stuck to the back of the log too, it was because of the end switch that had taken place to cheat.

By the end of the season,the young man was asking fewer questions every morning and Daddy said he was doing okay for a kid.

One thing I remember Daddy telling Momma was about the kid making bad decisions with the men and the business. It was clear that he had tried to help the kid, and he wanted him to do well for his father and family who were counting on him. He could tell the kid was under great pressure to make money and the kid would sometimes make bad decisions on how to do things. Daddy could only stand by and watch as he could do no more than make a suggestion in the ear of the kid.

Daddy ran out of patience though late in the season and pledged to never go back. The kid apparently turned on Daddy when some of the other men convinced him that it was Daddy who was manipulating him. The kid put him in a work station where he would make very little money as if he were a new hand with no experience. Needless to say, we left shortly after and headed back for sunny California. It was early April anyway and the logging operation would soon shut down.

The one comment Daddy made over and over on that trip back still rings in my head today: "The power of authority, alone; gives you the right to bad decisions."

It took me many more years to understand what he was talking about. As I said earlier, the older I get the smarter my Daddy gets.

CHAPTER EIGHT

Sometimes At Christmas

In about 1943, we had moved to Chowchilla, California, and were living next to a dairy where Daddy had picked up a job for the winter.

World War Two was in full swing and milk products were in high demand from the government. Not only did our troops need dairy products, but the government was helping our allied countries with food supplies as their agriculture industry had been all but destroyed by the war.

The Government was paying top dollar for dairy products and many of the small farms were taking full advantage of the money to expand their operations and buy more cows and land. All of that translated into the need for more help of any kind.

Many of the men had gone off to war and help was badly needed in these areas of agriculture, so even Daddy could get one of the jobs.

The men and women who were of able body were taking jobs in the major industrial areas of the country - one reason was for the money but just as important at that time, was that working in anything to do with the war industry was considered very patriotic.

As it was, the dairy had housing available for its workers and we had plenty of raw milk to drink and use from the milking every day. Daddy would let us kid's come over to the milking barn and get a bucket of raw milk every day when he was working.

Momma and Little Granny would go right to work on the milk as soon as we got back with it. They would separate the cream and butter. The butter was used for cooking and the cream was stored in the shared ice box by all the ranch hands families. Each family had a small section for their items and everybody was very respectful not to take anything that was not theirs.

I remember all the times I wish we had milk or butter to use and did not have it available, so we made sure we did not waste a drop of it when it was available.

The baby of the family, Bella, had it better than any of us did when we were real young, so she was really fat as a baby from all the dairy milk. Daddy would tease with all of us and tell us he was fattening her up because he was going to sell her by the pound at the Livestock Yard over by Highway US 99. It was a good time for our family because of the food available at the ranch.

Daddy worked for a man there by the name of, Jimmy Smith. Everybody just called him "Smitty." Smitty was good to us, and he knew Daddy was letting us get the bucket of milk every day but never said a word about it because he knew we were a family of seven kids. Besides, he knew if he put a stop to it, we would probably resort to stealing it. No reason to make someone a thief if you don't need to.

There were a couple of times Smitty helped me get the bucket over the wire fence and back to the cabin. He would say something like, "Let me help you with that bucket of water young lady," and then he would smile real big as he waited for me to climb under the wire before handing it back to me.

Smitty had kids too. He would bring them around the farm to help with weekend and holiday work so the other men could have a little time with their own families. I think the young boy was named Jimmy too - he was about the same age as me and he looked just like his dad. He acted the same too. He had the same walk and he would do and say the same thing as his dad, the whole time looking up at him for approval.

Daddy would just laugh at the young boy as he watched them and call the young boy, "little boss." I don't think they had much more than us to live on because Jimmy was wearing pants full of holes, and shoes to match.

Everybody was just trying to make it, and raise families, at a time when it was more than difficult to do. It was not just a matter of not being able to afford things; it was a matter of things not being available at any cost. The war took everything that it could get its hands on, and we were made to do the best we could with what was left.

I remember it as a time when so many others were again short of food and we had fallen into a place that gave us enough for at least one good meal a day. We didn't have any money to speak of, but the farm provided us with some vegetables and a small amount of meat as part of the pay for working.

We had arrived there early enough in the season to get some canned vegetables and dried fruits from the summer garden on the farm. Many of the families, who had been living there for some time, tended to it and shared what they grew there with all the others.

We were very lucky to get so much and not have to go out looking for food every day. I don't remember ever having to eat small birds or collard greens the whole time we lived there. It was so very nice for a change.

I got to go to school for awhile as well, and it seemed like heaven not having to work out in the fields all day and even better than that, no deep snow to walk through to the outhouse every morning.

By the way, if someone forgot the toilet ring out in the outhouse at night, and it wasn't sitting next to the wood stove, you would have to sit on a cold or even frozen ring in the morning, everyone would try to hold out until

someone else finally had to give in and be the first to use that icy cold ring and warm it up. Our mantra was, "bring the ring" in by the fire at night. We won't even get into not having soft cushy toilet paper like we do today.

We were so lucky in a way, because of Daddy's missing hand, he would not have to go to the war. We would think about that as we listened to the radio at night and hear of all that was going on oversees with other men. I would see Daddy quickly look down at his stump when they would tell of all the lives lost and families' devastated. The missing hand may have been a blessing for that reason, but it was a curse for so many other reasons. If the war would have taken Daddy, I am sure he would have gone like all the others. He was patriotic and afraid of nothing; he was as fierce as any other man.

We began to hear on the evening radio programs of all the Government was going to do for the men and women who were away at war. I guess we had not really thought much about Christmas as so many of them had come and gone with no real difference for the day. Had it not been for some of the things the local Church was providing, I am not sure we would have given much thought to the day?

It's not that we did not believe in God, we just seemed to spend our days trying to figure a way to eat.

The church had been so good to us, and especially to me with the dress and shoes. It is just that we did not make a big deal out of it, because we had nothing to celebrate as far as we could tell.

For so many years, we had nothing to give each other and we did not feel as though we were really part of any community. The rest of our family was scattered all over the country trying to survive from years of the Depression and we were kind of alone. The nine of us was all we had. When Little Granny was with us, we had all the family we needed.

It was hard all those years watching a celebration come and go and not understanding what it was all about and why we were left out of it.

I was just a young girl and wondered what the big deal was. I had been made welcome at the church in Visalia and went to Sunday school a couple times, but don't remember too much about what the reason for all the celebration was. Momma and Daddy did not even celebrate birthdays as I remember. I was not even sure what my birth date was until I was about fifteen years old.

I think it was just a few days before Christmas that year, Smitty was coming to all the cabins and handing packages out to everyone. All of us kids were sitting out in front of the cabin when he came up to ours and asked if he could talk to Momma and Daddy. We fetched them real quick and both of them came outside to see what Smitty wanted.

We were all pretty curious to know what was in those packages he was giving out and wondered why he was doing it. Smitty was real nice as he talked to them and kept asking if he could give us kids something. Momma told him to go ahead and give us what he wanted.

Smitty motioned with his hand to come over with him, to someone sitting in his car. Pretty soon here came a lady and Jimmy, Little Boss, out of the car. The lady was carrying a big paper bag, and Jimmy a handful of candy sticks. He ran over to us, and with a big smile, he started handing out those candy sticks to each of us kids.

We were all so excited with the candy that we just ran off to eat it without ever seeing what Mrs. Smitty had in the bag.

I ate some of my candy stick and stuck the rest of it in my pocket, Jimmy came running up swinging a stick around over his head like a sword. I took off running, and he must have chased me for a mile before he quit and ran back to his car because his dad, Smitty, was calling for him to come back.

After they left, I went back to the cabin to find Momma with that paper bag open on the table. She was sorting through all kinds of canned goods and what looked like a big chunk of meat of some kind.

Daddy was admiring all the things and kept saying how good those people were for doing that for us. He said, "we are not even kin and look at all they did."

I remember some of it, but couldn't get my mind off how good that candy stick was and still enjoying what was stuck to my teeth. It was a treat we did not enjoy often as children, and when we did, we would hide to eat it so the others would not try and take it from us. I was thinking Jimmy was coming to get my candy stick, but I guess he just wanted to play.

In those days, everything was rationed because of the war effort. For someone to give you some of what they got in their ration was pretty special. They had a family to take care of too and may have given up some of their Christmas dinner for us.

It takes special people to do such a thing; I have never forgotten the generosity shown us by the Smith family of Chowchilla, California.

The next day we went over to their house in town with a load of firewood from the ranch to help unload it. While we were there, Jimmy took me inside their house to show me their Christmas tree. I told him I had never seen one in person.

I had seen some pictures in books and the window of some stores, but we had never had one and all the folks in the camps did not put one up. I was glad to see what one looked like in someone's house.

We went in the front door, and he pointed over to the corner of the room, "there it is" he said. I looked at it for a minute and kind of laughed because it was not like the trees I had seen in the pictures.

I asked what it was, and he said it was their Christmas tree and that he and his Mom had spent all day putting decorations on it. He told me how much work it was to decorate and how happy he was about having one.

I was still wondering what he was so excited about, it was kind of ugly and funny looking but it seemed to be real important to him. He said his dad made it for them from what he got at work because they could not afford to go to the mountains to get a tree because of the gas rationing.

I told him it was nice and went back to help unload the firewood around the back of the house so we could get back to the farm. I was not too impressed with the Christmas tree and wanted to tell Daddy about it as soon as we left.

As soon as we took off in the truck back to the ranch I started to tell Daddy about the tree when he told me he had already seen it. He told me he had already seen it when he was there delivering the last load of wood. He asked if I wanted to know what Christmas was all about.

I think I asked for him to tell me about the tree first, and then I would listen to him tell me about the rest of it. Daddy laughed for a moment and told me he had helped Smitty pick up and load the stuff they had used for the tree. He said everybody was very poor and we had to use what we could find to make Christmas trees. Daddy said we never had a tree because it was too much trouble and he did not want to make a problem with cutting down someone's trees for it. He said all a Christmas tree did was keep someone from a nice load of firewood later on.

I asked what kind of tree Jimmy had, and Daddy again laughed for a second and said," it's not really a tree Betty Girl, they just made one out of it". Again I asked what that funny tree was made out of. He told me," it was three tumbleweeds all stacked on another and covered with ribbons and pinecones". He said they must have sprayed it with some white and green paint for the color so it did not look like tumbleweeds.

He told me him and Smitty had looked along the fence for the tumbleweeds with Jimmy a few days ago because they could not go get a real tree. He wanted to have something for them because it would be another year without presents for the kids.

A tumbleweed tree and presents was something I had never even heard of before. I had never been given a Christmas present or even heard of some one who had. I was always told by my parents that it was all done for, "the rich folks."

I was getting a little older and the other kids were too. We were starting to ask questions about Christmas, birthdays, presents and why we never did any of that.

I can tell you Daddy had plenty to say about all the present giving and who that was for. He told us we did not do it because he was not going to do what the government wanted because he had already given the State of Missouri his left hand and that is all they were going to get from him.

That was the end of the talk about presents.

I asked what the Christmas holiday was all about and why people celebrated it like they did. He said he would tell me what he knew, and I would have to go see the Preacher for the rest of it.

In typical Daddy fashion, he told me about some of it but was quick to get to the end of the explanation. He said, "It is about the birth of Jesus and this is the day they think he was born on. The churches celebrate it with presents and food just like they did when he was born a long time ago. Everybody believes in God and we have to be good so we don't go to hell." That was it from Daddy. He told me to go to church if I wanted to know anymore about it than that.

Well, that is exactly what I did and I am glad I did. It has given me hope many times through my life when I needed something to hold onto and when all the people I trusted seemed to betray me.

The world will consume you if you let it; the world only cares about what it can do for this time and has no concern for the time we will spend in eternity. I think I can learn to live with some challenges in this life and wait for the next part; that is where it is suppose to get really good ya know!

We did in fact celebrate Christmas with a beautiful dinner, one like I had never had before in my life. A big ham to eat with canned fruit for dessert was one of the most special meals we ever had as a family and the best meal this family had ever seen. We have the Smith family in Chowchilla, California to thank for it.

I still thank God every day for all they were to my family so long ago.

Jimmy showed up a few days later with his dad and was there to help load a truck that was coming out to the farm to collect scrap metal for the war effort.

Scrap metal drives was important to all of us and it was mandatory for this small community to be part of the effort. Everybody on the farm had been working to pile up old scrap metal from all over the community into a driveway out front of the milking barn so the big truck could get right up next to it for loading.

As we waited for the truck, we all talked about the dinner we had and how good it was. We were still eating some of the canned goods, and Momma was making soup from the rest of the ham. We were bragging about having so much food, we were still eating from the same dinner a few days ago, that was a first for us. We had never experienced leftovers!

The truck arrived and was pretty full already as it backed up to our pile of scrap. All of us got busy working to load the metal scrap when the driver started talking to Smitty and looking around at all the kids helping load the truck. Smitty was telling him how all of us had worked so hard to collect and pile all of the metal up to help, kids included.

The driver was asking about Christmas and the holidays with Smitty when he looked at us kids and asked what we had received for Christmas from Santa Claus. We just looked at Daddy and asked who Santa Claus was and why he would give us anything?

The driver looked a little puzzled when we did not know who he was talking about and waited for Daddy to answer him. Smitty jumped in and said we were not able to give any of the kids presents this year but we all had a nice dinner.

The driver did not say anything and went back to work loading the scrap.

We finished loading the truck and most of the kids had already scattered to go play or back to their cabins while we finished loading the last of the pile. The driver told Smitty and Daddy to help him up in the back of the truck. Both of them jumped up in the back to help arrange what we had thrown onto it.

Jimmy and me started walking off too when the driver asked us to wait for a minute. He said he needed some more help. For me it was always the same thing, everybody else is able to leave and go play or rest I am stuck working. It was not fair.

I was not going to complain and get in trouble with Daddy, so I just stayed and helped a little longer. All we were doing was moving metal around on the back of that truck and it made no sense to me, but we did it. Jimmy was really pulling and pitching stuff around when he stopped and called to me.

He was pointing at an old bicycle lying down under the other stuff. It was piled up pretty high, but we could see what it was. There were no tires on it. I guess they were salvaged for the rubber effort and it was just the frame, handlebars and the metal wheels. No seat and no chain, but it was as close to a bike as I had ever seen.

We went back to work and kept an eye on that old bike as we worked. We were talking about it and watching as the others were just walking right on top of it.

"All done and thanks," said the driver as the others jumped off the back of that truck onto the ground. Jimmy and I were still keeping an eye on that bike when the driver told us to jump down off the truck.

I tell you it was hard to just leave it behind because I had always wanted to ride a bike. It did not look like it was going to happen, even with a bike right under my feet.

Again we hear, "come on now kids I have a lot to do, let's go." Well that is it, I looked over at Jimmy and he was kind of crying as we jumped down walking away back to the barn where his dad was already standing waiting for us.

"Hey kids, come back here a minute. You left something," said the driver. As I turned around, the driver was holding that old bike up with one hand and waving at us with the other. "Come on," he said. We took off running over to him at the back of the truck like he was handing out gold. He said, "I think the war can be won without this one bike".

I guess he had been watching us look that old bike over and found out from Smitty and Daddy that we did not get any Christmas, so he was giving all us kids the bike for a present. I think they had us get up in the back and help move some stuff so he could get to it. Smitty and Daddy were in on it but never said a word as we worked to help uncover it a little.

We got up to that bike, got a hold of it and started fighting over who would push who first."Merry Christmas" he said, as he jumped off the back of the truck to get on with his work.

Daddy yelled out to him, "thank you sir." He replied back, "merry Christmas to you and yours. I think the war can do without that one old bike."

How about that, my first Christmas present and I just found out about Christmas a few days ago. I was thinking this God guy works pretty fast and I don't even remember meeting him. It's his birthday and he is giving me a present. WOW!

I pushed and shoved until I got the first ride on the bike. I think it was because Smitty told Jimmy, ladies first. I didn't know what that meant, but he got off and let me on.

There was no chain, so we could only push each other around in that dirt driveway. Oh yeah, did I mention it did not have any tires so we just rode it right on the metal rims.

The metal rims were digging into the ground and made it hard to turn; every time you tried to turn, it would dig in the dirt and throw you over on the ground like it was bucking us off.

We were all laughing as we watched each other go down the driveway with a good push just to end up on the ground at the bottom of the driveway next to the barn.

Once Jimmy was going too fast and there was no way to stop. He and the bike went right into the side of the barn. What a bang as he crashed and fell over right where the water washes out from the floor of the barn. I guess you know what he had all over his side when he got up?

Smitty came out to see what all the noise was. We were all running to hide because we thought we were in trouble for Jimmy running into the side of the milking barn. When he saw Jimmy, he went to laughing and calling for the other men to come have a look. I don't think Jimmy cared at the time, but I think he did later as dad sprayed him off with the cold water and then made him strip off all those clothes before he let him in the car for the ride home that evening.

We had the best time on that old bike all winter. We would hide it to make sure someone didn't steal it like it was a new bike or something.

Even though you had to stand up on the peddles to ride it because of the missing seat, it was a great time and we had endless hours of fun on that old bike. Each of us treated that bike like it was our own and made sure other kids from the nearby farms got a ride on it too.

We would act like we had to ride it in secret. Every time a car came down the road, we would hurry to hide it and wait until we thought it was safe to bring out again. We thought someone would report us for having it and not turning it in for the scrap drive as required.

We all got more than we expected that Christmas, a great dinner and a bike. It was the best Christmas ever.

There were a lot of things going on in our lives at that time and so many things we did not understand about what was going on in the world. I was just a kid, and did not understand everything the war was about and why we were fighting. I knew it was important because everything you heard on the radio or did seemed to have something to do with the war.

If it was that important in that small part of the world, then it must be important everywhere else too.

Chowchilla was good to us, but as always we moved on after winter in search of the work out on the road, Daddy complained about all the travel and where we would have to live. The pull was too strong for him to resist, setting out on the road each year in search of new work no matter how good we had it where we were.

I guess Daddy felt like no one could keep him. He had to always be on the move. That was his freedom and we were made to go along with it all of those years. He never stopped moving, his entire life was on the road, never settling down. I don't remember him ever living in one place more than a year, even when he got very old. He was a rambler at heart.

After we left Chowchilla, I wondered about that family, the one who had been so good to us when we were there. Smitty, Jimmy, his Momma and all those folks at the church down on Robertson Boulevard where I first went to church and learned about the birth of Jesus Christ; Christmas.

I thought about that tumbleweed Christmas tree in their front room and how proud Jimmy was to have it all decorated.

The bag of food they brought over to us and that darn bike was still stuck in my head. Especially about fighting Jimmy over that old rusted bike, as we pulled it back and forth and were trying to be the first to ride it.

Jimmy all covered in cow poop when he fell over in it by the barn and how we all laughed. I did not have a care in the world on that day.

Sometimes at Christmas, I pray for that family and what they meant to us on that day. What it meant to me the rest of my life. I wanted to be like them when I grew up and help others who were in a bad spot, just like we were. I often wondered why they would help us, someone who was a stranger to them and not even kin. I found the answer one day when I was reading my bible; here is what I found.

It was done for reasons I did not understand at the time, I do now!

Hebrews 13:16

Do not neglect to do good and to share what You have, for such sacrifices are pleasing to God.

CHAPTER NINE

The War To Me

I turned six years old in December of nineteen forty one, just three days after the attack on Pearl Harbor. "Happy Birthday Betty Girl" was not spoken on that day. As I remember it, the words never came that day because the entire nation, heck, the entire world was still in shock. Even at six, I had some understanding that something very horrific had happened to us.

Our family and everybody else in the camp were sitting in front of the radio for several days without ever turning it off. If you tried to speak, you were hushed pretty quickly by someone. It seemed as though this was something that was so important you could not break away from it long without missing something; all of the men and women were listening and had a concerned look on their faces as they spoke in hush tones with each other.

The accounts of the attack were talked about over and over and with every bit of new information came a renewed anger of what had happened from all who listened.

This, of course, played out all over the country in homes and camps where people gathered to listen and console each other. The news was much slower to come, then what we receive today with all the technology, but it still had a devastating impact all the same.

It was a few days later, I think on my birthday that the President gave a speech to all of America about what had happened and what we were going to do about it.

Momma and Daddy took the time to talk with all of us as we would hear of the events of that day, December 7, 1941, to explain what all of it meant to us, our family. I was afraid of what happened there and wondered if we were all going to be killed the same way. The same as all those men and women in Pearl Harbor, Hawaii.

We all listened closely as Daddy told us about other wars and how America had won each of them because we would not be defeated by anyone, ever. It gave us some comfort to hear this from our Daddy, and Momma seemed to believe it too.

Little Granny was with us at this time and she talked about her childhood and how we defeated all who came against us. She told us how we defeated the Nazis and the Koreans too. She told us not to worry, we are a strong nation and she knew the President would do the right thing.

I know they were just trying to help us not be so scared and we counted on it as kids.

It was not long before we started hearing reports about men and women asking how they could sign up with the military to go fight the Japanese for doing this to us. It was being reported that long lines were forming outside of Government buildings all over the country by men and women who wanted to join the military and fight back. I remember the talk of the Government trying to set up ways to get people registered and how it might take months to get ready. People would not wait for months, they wanted action; now.

I was trying to understand what it meant to join the military and what it would be like to go fight.

All I knew about fighting was what I had seen in the camps we lived in, but those were drunken brawls and kids fighting. I wondered how we could defeat anyone who attacked us like they did, after hearing all the stories coming over the radio, the reports talked about bombs, gun fire and thousands of men killed in sunken ships.

To a little kid and one who had not been to school much, it was all strange to try and understand. It was a little exotic too. Go to a distant place, see other countries, meet others from all over the world and fight together. Why not? We fought in the camps all the time so why not do it somewhere in a foreign country. It was kid thinking, not understanding how so many would have to die to do just that. It was not exotic at all, it would be devastating.

Daddy would tell us stories almost every day about people he knew that had signed up to go fight the war. There were recruiting stations springing up all over the place. Every little town had a Recruiting Station for folks to come to and get information on how to sign up for military service.

We would see long lines outside the buildings and around the corner waiting to get inside. It seemed like it was that way every day as we drove by on the way to school.

I started to worry about Daddy signing up and leaving us alone as we drove by and was worried that Curtis would go to. I had no idea who could sign up and go and, of course, it made me afraid of how we would survive without Daddy.

All of us kids started to ask questions of Momma and Little Granny. We wanted to know more about the possibility of Daddy and Curtis leaving to go to the war. We thought of Smitty and Jimmy back in Chowchilla too.

Momma told us Daddy would not have to go because of his missing hand and that Curtis was too young to join and not to worry about any of the family leaving. It was comforting to a little kid to know all of us would be staying together.

We were living in Visalia, California when the war started. People began to change and seemed to be angry all the time, cursing the Japanese people openly in public. Picture boards were going up all over town with all kinds of information and pictures of American Servicemen in uniform. "Join Now For The Defense Of America And All We Stand For", the signs read.

At our camp there were Poster Boards where we used to get our information on things about the work location for the next day or wages for the next section of crop to be picked. These boards were now telling everybody where to sign up and how to do it. They said, "Help Win The War, Sign Up Today To Do Your Part".

I would watch bus loads of men leaving every day. I could see the bus station across the street from the school out of the window of our classroom. I would watch as each man walked onto the bus and continue to watch as it drove off out of sight around the corner.

Women and kids were left standing there, waving and crying as the bus pulled away and around the corner out to the highway. Many of the women would still be there waving long after the bus had left their sight. Our Teacher Mrs. Brenda, would always tell us how important it was for them to go.

Some of the kids would point to men getting on the bus and say it was their neighbor or someone their dad worked with and that they had been to their house or played with their kids on a baseball team.

I remember one little boy who was crying as this man got on the bus. He did not move away from the window as he watched the bus drive away. That boy kept calling out to him; it was his dad. Mrs. Brenda picked him up and held him tight, turning him away from the window. She told him it would be okay and kept telling him she was sorry. She said, "I'm sorry, I'm sorry "son". It will be okay and I love you. Your Daddy will be okay. He wanted it this way." They cried for sometime before another teacher took the rest of us outside to play.

I wondered why his dad had not given him a penny to put in his shoe too. I stood there and thought about that penny my Daddy had given me, as I pressed it against my foot. It would bring me good luck and my Daddy would not have to go away like his dad. That penny gave me comfort. Every time I watched those men getting on that bus, I would make sure I could feel that penny pressing against my foot inside my shoe. My Daddy's promise to me would keep us together, safe.

I was still a little afraid and would watch the bus station every day to make sure my Daddy was not getting on the bus, then start watching at the end of the school day for him to pull up in front of the school. If he was even a few minutes late I would start to worry; worry that I missed him get on that bus. Then I would scold him for being late picking me up.

It was a traumatic time for us and, of course, there was nothing kids could do but wait to see if it would next happen to their family. Each day was another day to worry and watch; I am glad we were at a farm that was familiar to me.

Fortunately, the ranch Daddy was working at that winter was one we had been to during many previous winters. Daddy was the foreman at the time because the man who was doing it before had left for the war. This gave Daddy the use of the farm truck and that is what he used to take me to school and pick me up each day.

This also meant a better cabin for us and some more money too. That never really worked out though because Daddy said the organization that owned the ranch was a "bunch of pencil necks" that did not know how to run a farm. They were "a bunch of bankers who only cared about the money, not people."

We started to eat a little better for awhile because of so many men leaving for the war, that meant better jobs and better pay was being offered to those who stayed.

As was usual for Daddy, there would be trouble with him and the owners of the ranch. As usual, we loaded the car and headed for greener pastures. No more school for a while but I didn't mind because it would mean I did not have to worry every day and watch for Daddy to make sure he did not get on that bus to the war.

We had to slow down our travel though because of all the gas rationing that was going on for the war effort. We had to go to a county building as we traveled to report for the census. They wanted to know how many people are in our family and where we lived so we could get our new Gas Coupons.

Each person got a coupon allotment no matter the age; we used the allotments for our travel and food. It could be a challenge at times getting the coupons, with us on the move all the time. We would have to wait for days for the government folks to verify who we were and it took them time to make sure we weren't trying to double dip on coupons. As it was, we had to turn in any unused coupons in the county in which they were issued, before the next county would issue new coupons from their county. It was a real mess for folks like us who always were on the move.

The folks at the gas stations and grocery stores were real sticklers about having us turn in the ration coupons with everything we bought.

It was not just gas and oil, but also sugar, tires, meat, cheese, butter, shoes, and just about everything else a family needed. You could forget anything

extra from the government people. They did not care if you did not have what you needed; it simply was not available it at any price.

We had been doing okay picking up and selling glass and the scrap-metal business was pretty good, too. If it wasn't nailed down, you better keep your eyes on it if my brother Curtis was around. He knew that selling scrap metal meant better food and, maybe, some meat with our beans - so he was watching all the time for opportunities to grab what he could.

We were able to sell some of our ration cards for the things we could not afford anyway and trade them for what we needed to keep moving - gas and oil. I think everybody was doing it because we had trouble trading at some gas stations. Many families had come through ahead of us, and the store-keepers did not want to trade anymore ration cards for sugar or tires - even at a very cheap trade rate.

We did not have to travel as much for work as we had in the past, with a shortage of men at home. Many women now were working in the war factories too, so that meant good farm job pickin's for us.

When men would see Daddy's missing hand, they would ask if he needed work. They knew he would not be going to war, and they might be able to hire him cheap, because of only having one hand with which to work. That never went well, as you might imagine.

The war was difficult for many people but it seemed to be better for Daddy and probably others like him who were experienced workers but had been pushed aside for 'able-bodied' men. See, at that time a disability meant you were less capable and could not work like other men and didn't have a chance for the job.

Daddy was turned down at one factory after another for jobs because of his missing hand. If he managed to hide it from them to get hired, as soon as they found out he would be fired and there was nothing he could do about it.There were no laws to protect him.

If he wanted to stay, they would make him work for less money than the other men. It is the same thing the big companies were doing to blacks, Hispanics and Women - lower wages for the same work. They had no way to do anything about it because the laws did not protect them. Nobody really cared about what minorities and the disabled wanted and – they were just exploited for company profit.

Because we had worked in the fields next to blacks, Hispanics, Women and other children most of our lives, we didn't see them as being different than anyone else. We all worked for the same wages, we all were dirt poor. Then, Daddy started talking to them about how unfair it was that some people made less money than others. We learned a lot about what had been going on - how business owners would pay less if you were handicapped, or in the minority.

This was a 'hot-button' topic that made Daddy really mad - but with no one to complain to, or anybody who cared enough to stand up for the underpaid workers, it was a losing battle and would have to be for someone else to fight. We usually would move on to find work elsewhere.

The entire nation was undergoing significant changes in how we worked and who was hired. Factories were popping up everywhere, and they needed people to build the machines and equipment needed for the war effort.

Momma would point at the lines of people outside the factories as we drove by, she was pointing at the women who were going to work. It was not just women - many children were being put to work in the factories, too. We were used to seeing kids in the fields because it was normal for women and young children to be working there, but the big factory jobs, they had only been for white men in the past.

To tell you the truth, I don't think Momma and Little Granny cared much for women working in the big mills and factories. They talked about how wrong it was for women and kids to do that kind of work. "It was man's work" Momma would say.

The war changed things, and they would never be the same. The attack at Pearl Harbor changed how we produced machines and who was needed to build them. We quickly became more industrialized. The change of social attitudes concerning women and children working in factories would take much longer.

The government was doing everything they could to convince every citizen that it would take more than military might to win the war. Everywhere one turned there was a poster or billboard with patriotic signs. Every radio broadcast talked about doing one's part, and every time we picked up our ration coupons we were reminded to shoulder our responsibilities for victory.

Many of the government employees from whom we had to pick up the ration coupons, would try to make Daddy feel as if he was shirking his civil duty because he was not in the military. Even when he showed them his stump, they seemed to imply that he did it so he would not have to go fight; if they only knew what kind of man Daddy was, they would never had thought him a coward. Daddy was a fighter – he didn't back down or run the other way even when it was foolishness or in drunkenness.

The war seemed to drag on for years, and it was a part of everything we did as a country united. It was impossible to escape the war hype, because it was in everywhere we looked and all that we heard. At times, I just wanted to escape the whole world - to be away from the pressure of patriotic propaganda.

It even was part of our everyday work in the fields - work harder, we were told, the boys in uniform are counting on you. With rationing, we were forced to stay longer in one place then we normally would have.

Some of the farms we normally would have gone to harvest were too far to travel with the coupons we had for gas. We wanted to go help farmers on our regular route, but it was impossible to get there with the gas rationing and other shortages of rubber for tires and food. Farmers had to look for local help, and they had to pay better wages to keep the help there. We saw many more young kids working in the fields than ever before - it was good for us because we were experienced and could pick much more than many of the newcomers who had little or no experience. All of a sudden Daddy was in demand.

The cost of everything had gone up and it became more difficult to get basic items for everyday living. Daddy had to resort to "horse trading." I remember Momma saying he wasn't too good at horse trading and always lost his shirt on the deals, but there was no other way to get some of the things we needed. Boy, we sure could have used "ol, Creekmore" about now.

The ration coupon only gave you the right to buy a set amount of particular items - you still had to come up with the money to pay for the item. As prices climbed, on just about everything, we relied more on what we had done in the past - trading and stealing. It seemed that, things only would be better for us a short length of time and then it was right back to hot, cold, hungry and tired - it was our way of life.

As I look back at some of the things that happened at that time, I know I was hugely affected, even as a young girl, on how I started to see my life. Momma and Little Granny did not like women working in factories, however the idea of it made me think that maybe I could finally feel equal to other people. Much of my life I had to struggle for equality and fairness, that I felt others didn't. I was a poor, uneducated women living in a man's world of which we were reminded nearly every day. It took a war to begin the slow change to women gaining a degree of equality with men.

I found myself in trouble over the years because I would not accept someone else trying to make me into who they wanted me to be. I think my station in life as a woman gave people the idea they could do what they wanted to me.

As a little girl, I didn't know how to be my own person in a way that others would accept. Much of the time my behavior appeared as rebellion against family, playmates and others, because I was unwilling to accept our culture's in equality to women, children and minorities. If women continued to accept being forced to the back seat in every aspect of their lives and - with plenty of white men to work the factories - blacks, Hispanics and disabled people just accepted what they were given, nothing would change for any of us.

Change did begin when women, blacks and Hispanics started to demand better wages and working conditions. Bankers and factory managements tried to make us appear unpatriotic and selfish because of the sacrifices the men in uniform were making oversees. It was as if anyone who wasn't a soldier should expect to be given less, and accept it, because only soldiers were important and necessary to win the war.

It all came to a head when new propaganda posters started showing up in factories. They were making up their own instead, of using government issued posters, in order to keep people working for less and less.

Wages were controlled by corporations. The government couldn't keep up with the mass of people working in factories to assure fair and equal wages were being paid. Needless to say, nearly all who worked in factories were cheated. If you wanted to keep a job, then you better keep your mouth shut or they would replace you with one of dozens of people standing outside desperately wanting work. Trust me, management was about profit, not patriotism.

In 1943, the blacks in Detroit and Hispanics in Los Angeles started rioting over unfair labor practices. They demanded better wages, equal wages, and better working conditions. They wanted fairness in how people were hired and fired so they could get and keep jobs just like whites. People were beginning to organize and protest. It was a struggle fought across America – many people lost their lives over the next couple of decades in the battle for equality.

Do we have equality for all, yet? I'm not sure. The fight will continue, as long as we allow those in control to twist words like patriotism for increased stockholder profit.

Because of fear, Daddy worked in deplorable conditions and kept his mouth shut while he was at work, but we would hear all about it when he got home. That was when Daddy started drinking more because of all the pressure. I think some of it was fear about the war, too. Everyone on the planet was affected by the war, and no one escaped its cost. Those costs have been paid out over generations and, some are still suffering that cost through the loss of those who were killed as a result of war. Those lost can never be replaced and many were never accounted for. Those families still wonder, still miss and still grieve for their loved ones.

Let me tell you about the cost as a child traveling on the long dusty roads of this great country – how sacrifice and pride that are somehow bound together. We are all "ONE NATION' no matter how we are divided, we are one, "AMERICANS".

As I think about it now, I am glad I grow up in the era I did. I reflect on how God kept us children safe from all the evil going on around us in the rest of the world. The war was terrible. It devastated the people fighting it; their families back home waiting and wondering if their loved ones were okay, still alive, hurt or hungry. Entire countries were leveled and entire families were lost in the fighting. Entire families!

I guess what I want all those who lost their lives, their families, to know is that it was worth it. You gave kids like me a chance to be a kid, to ride old bikes and laugh at each other, to play and eat the best dinner of our lives. I know the great sacrifice this entire country made to remain free, and the great advancements in industry, technology and society that they protected with their service. Always remember - nothing is free - everything has a cost and someone paid that cost for me; for that reason, I am eternally grateful.

Japanese Admiral Yamamoto of the Japanese Military Forces Pacific Division in charge of the fleet that attacked Pearl Harbor credited with a comment, just after the attack, to his executive officers on the bridge of the aircraft carrier. I

think it sums up how we were perceived by the rest of the world at that time. It goes like this:

"I fear, all we have done is to awaken a sleeping giant, and fill him with a terrible resolve."

We had been in a great depression and the country was in bad shape - in too many ways to count. We were broke and had lost what our families had built for themselves over generations.

The attack gave us a rallying point and brought us back into one unified effort.

Now I know what Little Granny and Daddy were talking about when they said "we could not be defeated." We are Americans, in spite of all of our differences; we are united in the fight for freedom!

CHAPTER TEN

Runaway

There comes a time in everyone's life when we start to seriously consider and plan for independence. In looking back at my own childhood it was not hard for me to recognize why Midge and Donnie began to separate themselves from the family, especially Momma and Daddy.

Fights between the girls and our parents came more often, and began to create division in the entire family. It was hard not to get involved. Living in one-room cabins and working together all day in the fields, we had no time of our own and no place to escape our parents' suppressive conditions.

Midge and I had been very close through the years and had shared almost everything with each other. That started to change when she turned 16 years old. That would have been about 1946.

It seemed like Midge could make a problem out of nothing hoping to test Momma - to see if momma would let her do whatever she wanted, whenever she wanted. Midge quit going to school and work. She would not do chores in the cabin while we were out working in the field. When we would get to the cabin in the evening, Midge would be sleeping or gone. Momma would be so angry because Daddy began taking it out on the rest of us kids. Midge didn't seem to care anymore, about any of us.

I tried to talk to Midge but she wouldn't even want to talk to me. That was a very hard year for me as she claimed her independence from all of us. She no longer needed me but I was still in desperate need of her. She was my confidante.

I know Midge had been running off to town to meet up with boys during the day, because I saw them drop her off a couple times out by the road in the evening. I smelled liquor on her breath a couple times, too; I knew she was headed for trouble with Daddy when he found out.

I know Midge wanted more. More than Momma and Daddy could provide at the time. As I look back, I recall that she never was satisfied with what we did, where we worked, and she was ashamed of how we had to live.

The war changed things for us at times, but there was never enough money to allow us stay in one place all year, buy a house or anything of that sort. Daddy was pretty good at getting jobs and finding work when others could

not, but we still lived the same down trodden way. If there was extra money, none of us kids knew anything about it.

Our lifestyle was somewhere near the bottom of standards for most folks. We were never really accepted into any community, except to work in the fields –that's how it had always been for us. We were on the fringes of society - people didn't want to see us because it reminded them we were there, we existed.

Midge used this to her advantage and was able to move in and out of those small towns unnoticed and unapproachable. Midge was quiet most of the time because she had learned how to use her polio to get what she wanted. If she did not want to do something, all she had to do was tell Momma her legs hurt and act like she was having trouble walking. I think Momma knew what she was doing, but she also knew she could not make Midge do anything she did not want to.

All of us kids knew what she was doing, too, and we started to resent Midge for always being a baby and using her polio to get out of her share of the work. Midge didn't seem to care. She treated us like strangers, even after all the sacrifices we made for her all through the years. All of us had given her the best place on the mattress, the best place in the back of the car - with the most room. We bore her share of chores many times to spare her from pain. Now, we were getting tired of the constant complaining and arguing, about everything that happened, when she did not get her way. We felt she owed all of us something for all we had done for her, but it would never be repaid.

At the time, we were living in a small cabin along the Tuolumne River outside Modesto, CA. Midge had been gone for a couple days, and we were all worried about her. She had left for a day or so before, but she usually let me know when she would be back, not this time. There were lots of things to do in town, and it was common for kids to roam around Modesto and party. It had taken a hold on Midge as she found acceptance from the other kids there. She was experiencing her first taste of freedom and independence.

It was spring and the weather was mild, so she would stay out all night and drink while sitting along the riverbank. Midge was partying with some older men, and that concerned me. I told her she better watch out what she was doing and leave those older men alone. Well, she didn't listen to anyone, including me, and off she went. Many of the men coming back from the war were looking for young girls with whom to party and take advantage. She would do anything, to anybody, to be with them.

When it rained, Midge came back as wet as a stray dog and smelling like one too. I would ask where she had been, she would tell me how great it was staying out all night and whooping it up with all the local kids.

Midge would leave again as quickly as she came back and it became common that she was gone more then she was home. I was about 12 years old at the time, but I could see how it was bothering Momma. Midge was her oldest and had required the most attention over the years. Because of the polio, Momma was close to Midge and felt Midge needed her to survive. I'm not sure Momma had ever considered that Midge might leave the family and go out on her own -now it was happening and, none of us were handling it very well.

Midge was not making her exit to independence easy for any of us. I expected her to just not come home one day and that would be the last time I ever saw her. I think that is how I was learning to accept her leaving me.

I was hoping she would stay home for a few days because it had been raining nonstop for a week. I worried about her being out in the cold and wet weather because it seemed to cause her legs to get real stiff and increase the pain as reported by Midge in the past. Also, I had been missing her company.

That old cabin was not much, but it had a good wood stove in it to keep us warm and, there were no leaks in the roof. There never was enough room on the floor for the two big mattresses we made from Johnson grass along the riverbank earlier that year. It was a small cabin and we were a large family, we were used to being crowded though, it was normal.

A church had been helping with some food and clothes for us. Daddy was working for the local graveyard doing concrete work and building a brick wall. The money was good - it was pretty good for us anyway.

Midge kept talking about how she was missing out on this and that while she was at the cabin and not in Modesto, and how she needed to get out. I wanted her to stay because of the weather and drinking. She was hell bent on going to town to party with her new-found friends.

The bridge over the river had been underwater several times that week as the rain and snow melt from the Sierra Nevada Mountains made its way downstream in the Tuolumne River. The water was swift and deep, it was kind of scary. I knew the only other bridge over the river was several miles up the road, and was too long a way for Midge, because she usually set out on foot to get to town. I also knew she was dumb enough to try and cross that bridge no matter what the conditions. The water was over the road but the big concrete railing was just above the surface of the water and she had mentioned several times that she would consider walking or crawling on the wide railing to get across if she had to. Midge was a bit of a daredevil and she was also thick headed enough to try. If she could cross the river at the Santa Fe Empire Bridge, she would be in Modesto in a short time. Midge could not endure the long walk to the next bridge at Hatch road, because of the leg pain caused by polio.

I had gone with momma and daddy to town to pick up some food at the Baptist Church and only was gone about an hour. By the time we got back to the cabin Midge was gone, again. Momma said she probably was in the outhouse and would be back soon. The problem was, the outhouse was nearly underwater from high river water. I knew Midge wouldn't attempt going down to the outhouse – she didn't know how to swim, and the slick hillside down to the outhouse was a slippery trip even on a good day.

We waited for a long time for her to come back. I kept watching out the window because Daddy yelled at me for opening the door to get a look and in the process letting cold wet air into the cabin. I was worried she was going to try and cross the bridge and be swept away by the fast water.

After a while, I walked up to the Empire bridge to see if Midge was there waiting to hitch ride to town. If she saw our car coming up the road from town and did not want us to see her she would hide down over the hillside from us until we passed before she would climb back out looking for a ride to town. It was still pouring rain and cold-as-the-dickens by the time I got there.

Midge was nowhere in sight, so I just watched the water rush over the bridge. The water was running fast, and the roadway was completely covered. The only thing you could see was the bridge railing sticking up. I don't know how deep the water was, but there was no way someone could get across there, not even a car would make it without being swept away.

I sat there for about a half an hour, when a car stopped to look at the water level on the bridge before trying to cross. Two men got out to survey the water conditions and talked about how it was as bad as they had seen in recent years. I asked if it always was like this and they said, not always. They told me it was much too dangerous to attempt crossing when the water got to this level and the snow runoff was much too cold to endure for more than a few seconds. They said the water was so cold it was, "paralyzing". They added that they had just come from down river and it was not as bad at the higher Hatch Road Bridge in Modesto.

They were farmers from nearby Hughson and had lived there all their lives. They said they read in the newspaper about the flooding and came to see for themselves what it looked like. I told them I was worried my sister Midge may have tried to cross the bridge to Empire, because we could not find her back at our cabin. I told them about her polio, her weak legs and that she had talked about attempting to use the railing to crawl over to the other side of the river. I also told them she couldn't swim.

They said they had just come down the road from Modesto and didn't see anyone walking or hitching rides. They questioned why she would take off walking on a day when it was raining so hard. They asked why she might have tried to cross on the bridge rails that were sticking up just above the water surface. I told them she was a daredevil and thick headed at times and that she did not have good balance and would have fallen in if she had tried. I told them she had braces on her legs because of Polio and had to use a cane for balance. The top of the rail was wet and slick, too.

I ran home to tell Momma and Daddy that Midge was missing and I was worried she tried to cross at Empire Bridge. Daddy said not to worry and Midge would know better than to try crossing there. I went up to the hillside where we had been going to the bathroom to look for her, calling out her name several times with no response. I looked by the railroad trestle where we would sometimes sit and talk, but no luck there, either.

When I went back to the cabin crying, Daddy said he would take a drive along the road to see if he could find her. I got in the car and off we went down the long dirt road out to the paved road. By the time we made it up to the road by the bridge, we could see several other cars parked and looking at the water too. Daddy said we would stop and ask if anyone had seen Midge before we drove all the way to Modesto looking for her.

We stopped, got out and began asking if anyone had seen Midge and described what see looked like. Someone told Daddy that a young girl tried to cross there and was swept away by the fast water. They came out to see what was going on and see if they could help. Well, that's when all hell broke loose. We could see a police car coming up the road, and Daddy took off for the cabin. He didn't take time to tell me he was leaving and off he sped down the wet dirt road sliding all over and throwing mud up as the tires spun out.

I started crying and wondering if it was Midge that had been swept away trying to get to town, she was that determined at times and I knew it was possible. I was so mad about Midge running away and scared for her at the same time. I'm not sure what I was crying about most of the time, I was just scared for my sister.

The police car pulled up and started looking around and asking all the people there what they had seen. They would go back to their police car and talk on the radio, then go right back to looking up and down the riverbank and standing up on the bridge sides looking into the water and calling Midge's name.

Everybody was looking and running all over to see if they could find her. Daddy came back to get me and Momma was in the car with him. I ran over to the car and told them everybody was looking for Midge, but she was nowhere to be found. Daddy went over and talked to the police to see what they knew, and to tell them he was going to set out looking for her in Modesto.

They walked back to the police car and started talking on the radio, again. Momma and I sat in the car and waited. Some of the people there started to point at us as we waited - this made Momma cry even more. Some man walked right up to our car and started taking pictures of me and momma crying. I was so mad I just yelled at him to stop, and to go away.

Daddy did not like or trust Cops so I knew he would be mad about having to talk to them on top of being mad about Midge causing all this commotion for him. I was in a hurry to look for Midge but was not looking forward to Daddy making his way back to the car where me and Momma were sure to get a piece of his mind. We were sure it would cause daddy to reach for his whiskey bottle as well. This type of situation was never good for those around him when he was mad, and drinking.

We could see a police car on the other side of the bridge and some people were starting to look along the riverbank from that side too. By the time Daddy got back to the car there must have been a hundred people parked along the roadway and milling around by the bridge.

Daddy had to work around a little to get the car out of there because people were parking every which way with the road closed. We did get out after some cussing and yelling by daddy at some of the on-lookers about their driving abilities. We headed off for Modesto to see if we could find her, just in case she got a ride earlier. We drove all over South Modesto and the Crows Landing area looking for her because that is where she told me she had gone in some of her stories about partying.

We looked until dark, and then headed back to the cabin. We never did find her that night and nobody seemed to know who she was when we asked if they had seen her. Momma was pretty upset, and Daddy was too, but he looked more mad then afraid. I was crying when we got back to the cabin without Midge and not knowing where she was, everybody else started crying too. By this time daddy was tired from the search and pretty well drunk too.

Several times that evening the police car drove down the dirt road to our cabin, and every time Daddy would go see what they found out or if they had found Midge. Every time he came back in the cabin, we would all gather around to hear what Daddy found out.

I started to imagine her drowning, or hurt lying along the riverbank, wet, cold and scared. I could not get that picture out of my mind. I would try to not think about it, but it was too strong and, it was all I could think about. The pictures in my mind played over and over.

I wondered why Midge would try to cross that dang bridge with the water so high and fast. What was so important in Modesto that she would try to get across with her bad legs? I questioned myself – wondering if I had done enough to stop her. Why didn't I tell Momma or Daddy she was planning to leave, again, so they could make her go with us to the Church in Hughson? I wondered if I could have, or should have, tried to talk her out of going until the weather got better and the water was not so high. I know I could have stopped her if I knew she was going to try and cross that bridge even if I had to knock her down and tie her up in the cabin. There is no way I would have let her cross that river.

I was so mad at myself for not stopping her. Why did I let her do that? All the kids were crying and Momma was crying, too; Midge had been gone all day and now far into the night without a word from her. It was different this time then before because we were worried she was dead. It was a very difficult night for all of us. I'm not sure anybody slept. There was no place to escape and spend time alone thinking. It was a long night for all of us.

I wasn't looking forward to the morning, either; I no longer could hide my face in the blankets and cry. I would have to get out and look for Midge with the others and worry the entire time about whether or not it was my fault.

Midge and I had shared the same pair of shoes when we were younger and I helped protect her from kids in the camps who teased her because of the way her legs looked. She was not just my sister; she was my best friend too.

Early that next morning, I was walking on the dirt road when the police car was headed to our cabin once again. They drove past me with the tires spinning mud up from the wet road and didn't stop as they went by.

I watched as they continued slipping all over the rutted road down to the cabin. I turned around and ran back to see if they had found Midge, and if she was safe. Two officers got out and asked for Daddy. Without missing a step, I went running into the cabin. "Daddy, Daddy," I yelled. Momma was sitting on the edge of the bed and was talking to Daddy. Daddy was sipping a cup of coffee, just like he did every morning, leaning against the wall in the old wooden chair. They acted like nothing was wrong and barley even moved when I told them the police were out front.

Daddy slowly rolled his chair foreword and moved over to the door still holding onto his coffee cup. He never said a word as they told him they would need some more information about Midge and why she went missing. Neither of them ever broke a smile and it was all real serious. One of the officers kept resting his hand on his gun and looking at Daddy like he was some kind of criminal. I could see how mad that made him as he was all tense.

Daddy said he would see them later after he looked for Midge and would let them know if he needed their help. The police repeated what they already said about needing more information and then got back into their car. Daddy said something about them being pencil necks and closed the door. I was afraid that was the end of it, and no one would help us find Midge.

I told Daddy I was going out looking for Midge, and would be home later. I followed the police car down the drive. I could walk as fast as they were driving because of the slick driveway. I never looked over, I just walked on out beside them with their tires spinning the whole way; I kind of hoped they would get stuck and have to spend time digging out because they were mean to Daddy.

When I made it to the road, I looked down the road where the bridge was and could see cars driving over it. Some water was still on it, but it was nothing like it was the day before. Why couldn't Midge wait one more day to go over the bridge? One stupid day!

I took off across the bridge on foot with my shoes in my hand to keep they dry. Several people were standing around and one man was taking pictures of the bridge and high water. I didn't stop to talk - off I went through Empire on my way to Modesto.

I had no idea where to look for Midge, but knew if I found a wild bunch she would be close. I looked most of the day along the river and talked to everyone I found down there, with no luck. Some of the folks said they knew who she was, and that they were sorry to hear she had drowned. I would always repeat the same thing to them; "you don't know she drowned so don't say that".

I was so upset that most of the day is just a blur. I do remember telling all of those who had been partying with her how it was destroying our family, and that I was mad at all of them for doing that to her. It didn't occur to me that they had nothing to do with her running away, and they were just her friends. I was just very hurt and upset.

I made it back home late that evening and nobody was there when I got back. I wondered if they had found Midge and if she was at a hospital or something. I found out later that all of them had gone to the church for some offered food. Everybody would go because there was a good chance that you would get some kind of little toy or piece of candy if you were there. It also was a good place to glean information about what was going on and have a bit of gossip, Momma seemed to enjoy that type of thing.

Momma had assured me that the police were indeed looking for Midge even if it did not sound like they were - because of how Daddy was - and if anything turned up they would let us know. When they got home Momma told me someone had reported that a young girl had tried to cross the bridge and was swept away by the water early the day before.

Momma said the police were asking questions around town to see if any-one had seen the young girl who had been reported missing from the day before. Rumor was that some men who knew the young girl's sister had seen it happen and told their friends about it. They said they saw the event when they went out to inspect the high water over the bridge the morning before. They even described what she looked like with the leg braces.

The police received other reports about the incident and, they also were trying to locate the men who had been at the bridge that morning. Momma said the police were wondering why Daddy would not come and see them and wondered if he knew more than he was telling. They said Daddy was acting funny about the whole thing and because he did not come see them like they requested, they were even more suspicious of his behavior.

Daddy said he didn't need help from the pencil-neck police and wasn't worried about Midge anymore, because he was not going to worry every time she took off and didn't come home. That really was hard for me to hear.

I kept looking for her every day while Daddy was gone working. I looked along the riverbanks and around the bridge. I would call out to her and waited by the road, hiding in the trees in case someone dropped her off so I could tell her what was going on. I really wanted her to come back – I refused to give up on her.

Well, Daddy was right; he usually was about things like this. Midge came home a couple days later and just walked right in like nothing had happened. She acted like she was just coming back in from the outhouse; with a big grin on her face. She said some of her friends told her that we were looking for her and worried she had tried to cross the bridge and drowned.

Momma was glad to see Midge and hugged her and tried to talk to her, too, but Midge wouldn't talk about where she had been or how we had all gotten upset that she may have died.

She acted like it was no big deal and was rather amused about the whole thing laughing about how everybody was looking for her. I told her how scared I had been, and that I feared she had been swept away by the strong current and drowned. Midge laughed at me and said she wasn't crazy and would never try to cross that bridge the way the water was running that day.

I asked her where she went and she told me she hitched a ride to Modesto almost as soon as she got out to the road. She said a family saw her on the side of the road walking and stopped to see if they could help. She said she told them she had been kicked out of her house and was going to Modesto to stay with friends. She said they drove me right up to my friend's house and waited out front until I got to the door. She said they were a real nice family with two children and a nice car. She said it smelled real good and they were all dressed real nice, too. That would have been something to see - them all nice and clean and Midge smelling like a wet dog with dirty clothes.

I tried to talk to her more but she didn't care about everybody being upset and didn't care about how I cried out for her and kept looking for her after the others stopped. I told her I pictured her on the riverbank, cold, wet and hurting. She laughed at me and told me not to worry about her. She said, "I can take care of myself." I was devastated by her attitude and how she thought it was all a joke. I wondered if I would go look or even care next time she left without notice.

When Daddy got home from work and saw her at the cabin he never even said a word and acted like nothing had happened. I was very surprised to hear that when him and Momma went to the church for food that day, they went by and told the police she was back home safe. I am pretty sure he did it just to rub it in their faces that she had just ran away like he told them and that he had not caused her to go missing like they believed.

I was so mad at her and wondered why she no longer cared about any of us or how we felt. She stayed that way, uncaring and distant, with all of us until she left for good a few months later. She just left one day, like she had all the other times, and she didn't come back. I knew she was going to be gone for awhile - if not for good, because she took all her things with her, and a few things of mine, too.

None of us worried that time and, we didn't go look for her like the first time.

I knew she had been swept away by all that was different from how we lived. Midge was only 16 years old and had stayed home most of her childhood. She didn't go out much and didn't make friends easily, so it was a new experience for her to have her own friends and be out with people who accepted her, even with her funny looking legs. I guess her time to go had come.

Donnie was soon to follow Midge's migration from the family nest. She left one day and just never came back. When work ran out, we just moved on to the next place as we always had done and could only wonder where they were and what they were doing. Donnie was only 14 years old when she left, and I know she left with a soldier boy who was fresh back from the war and looking for a young wife. I had seen her hanging around outside the little Empire town bar with some guy a few times and saw him kiss her. I knew it wouldn't be long before she would run off.

Men returning from the war were well respected and, I guess, admired by everyone for what they had done. Many of them had new cars and money to burn. The president was promising good jobs for every returning serviceman and the government created jobs around the country to fulfill that promise.

There was talk on the radio about new houses being built for the returning soldiers to start and raise families. All the young girls dreamed about having a serviceman with money - a job and the offer of a new house. It was intoxicating to think about – that was all many of the young women wanted. After all those long years of scrap drives and coupons for everything from gas to sugar, the young women wanted better than their parents had been made to live with.

I remember how things changed for all of us after Midge and Donnie left. Daddy was becoming more distant and acted like he didn't care if we were there or not, I guess he was letting go of us. Momma still was the same and would take up for us, but Daddy would say things like, "I have my own life to live and I already gave all you kids some of the best years of my life -now I need to get on with mine."

Some other things also changed. If Little Granny was not with us, I got to ride in the front seat with Momma and Daddy. I was the oldest and I could make Curtis ride in back most of the time, until he would squeal to

Daddy, then I better move or I would get a back-hand for fussin' with "baby Curtis".

There was more room in the car and the cabin. We had a bit more to eat because there were fewer mouths to feed. I enjoyed that.

I had to work harder though, to make up for the money from the two who had left and were no longer helping earn money. I did it because I had to - it was expected of me and always had been. I did what I had to because I did not want a beating from Daddy, and he was giving them out a bit more regular after Donnie and Midge took off. Daddy was letting go of us but he was also driving us away with his drinking and beating of all of us, Momma included.

Riding in the front seat gave me access to some of what Daddy was thinking and why he believed what he did. Daddy liked to talk as we went down those miles and miles of road. I think it was the place he was most comfortable - on the road. He would talk in low tones to Momma as he drove along. I had with all the noise of the car and fussin' with the other kids never heard the talk as we drove along.

As we drove from the camp in Modesto to work the cotton fields in Bakersfield, I got to listen in as Momma and Daddy talked about Midge and Donnie leaving. Momma tried to stick up for the girls and said she understood what the girls were doing. Every time Momma would say why she thought they were better off, Daddy would raise his voice and tell her he thought they were tramps for doing what they did and, the way they did it. He said they should have been ladies and 'did it right' instead of running off with the first man that came along. Then, he would reach down and grab his coin pouch out of his pocket, rattle the little bit of change he had in it and say, "that's why they left, not love or respect."

Momma said she thought they left to follow their own dreams, just like Little Granny had told them too. Daddy said, "They are not chasing dreams. What they are chasing is their imagination. They will fail because imagination is wild and changes like the direction of the wind. They are not prepared to face the world on their own and make good decisions. To chase your dreams, you have to have a plan and then work hard to achieve it. They are just running away from what we have worked so hard to keep together. Chasing their imagination will always get in the way of their dreams because they will think they are the same thing. Don't confuse dreams with imagination, Momma."

I still wonder about that!

I didn't leave home until I was 18 years old. Was I chasing my dreams or my imagination?

I think we have to ask ourselves that question often, recognizing the difference between imagination and dreams. Thinking often about it helps us make the decisions that keep us on track with our dreams. I use imagination to fuel and excite my dreams, but I do not allow it to keep me from them.

Chapter Eleven

The Price Of Whiskey

Farm labor jobs were hard to find everywhere we went because farmers were using more machinery, now. Much of the work we had performed all those years could now be done in a day instead of a week by one hired man on a tractor. The days of a cabin being provided for field hands was coming to an abrupt end.

Because of the war, the nation had learned how to build equipment fast and efficiently. Many of the big outfits that had been making planes and bombs for the war were now building cars and farm machinery so we could feed a growing population cheaply. Along came the generation that would be known as "Baby Boomers."

Returning servicemen were doing just what they were told they could do - take factory jobs from the women who worked them during the war. "Rosie the Riveter" was out of work - back in the home. Her full time job was now having babies and taking care of them in that new house all of them had been promised.

Yep, those men were doing exactly what they were supposed to do. Again, Daddy was left to provide for his family with whatever job he could find for a man with one hand. Daddy sometimes was asked if he lost the hand in the war as the men would look at him with great respect and admiration, then he would tell them he lost it working for the State of Missouri when he was young. It seemed as though they no longer had any desire to even talk with Daddy, and of course, no job was offered, either.

Daddy was having a very hard time with work so difficult to find, so we headed for home territory and family. We bounced around Arkansas, Missouri and Oklahoma for awhile. Daddy picked up whatever work he could and he sometimes lied to get work, telling them he was back from the war.

Many young men were coming back with the same kind of problem my Daddy had suffered - men missing hands, arms and legs. Many of the men were not able to do the work of those who were able bodied, so they too had a hard time finding and keeping jobs. Unfortunately, many of them turned to drinking liquor to deal with it.

The Government was working to assist all the men who were disabled - but this was a new program for our country - helping people injured in a war. It was taking more time than people could wait. A hungry belly will only wait so long before it starts to look for food other ways.

We were in Dumas, Arkansas, living in a Federal Work Camp. Many living there were men just like Daddy. It seemed to bother Daddy that all of them got Government money on which to live, but because he lost his hand blasting tree stumps for the state prior to the war he got nothing but a lifetime of heartache and resentment. It sounded like this, "Where did you lose your hand sir? When he told them it was not from the war, he was told "Sorry we're not hiring."

As you can imagine, Daddy fell in with the malcontents and drinkers. He started to drink more than I ever remembered, and he became abusive not only to Momma, who he beat often to, as he put it,"keep her in line." He also began to beat us kids too for stupid stuff kids do.

All of us would try to stay away when he was at the cabin and not give him reason to beat us. The Federal Work Camps had strict policies about alcohol and drinking at the camps. If you were caught, you could be kicked out immediately, and not ever be allowed back in that camp.

The Federal camps were very nice with a big cabin for each family, shower and indoor toilet close by for all to use. We had electricity and running water in a sink in the small kitchen. It was quite nice in comparison to what we had lived in over the years. We did not want to mess that up with Daddy getting caught with liquor.

We would look for his stash and try to hide it away so he couldn't drink at the camp. He and the other men would go off, drink and fight somewhere else and come home late with all kinds of wild ideas about what their families should have been doing while they were gone. We were not the only ones being abused by our fathers, we kids would talk during the day; all of us were scared and afraid we would be thrown out by the man who ran the camp, if he found out about the drinking. He was a no nonsense kind of man, but always very friendly, as I remember. He allowed us kids to play with the water buckets and throw water at each other without getting mad. He knew we were just being kids.

Rent was $1.75 a week and had to be paid in cash. It was hard to come up with sometimes, but we somehow managed. Some of the work Daddy was getting was paid to him in food and the rent had to be cash. Unfortunately, most of the time it fell on me to do what work I could to get cash for rent.

102

I was doing housework for a couple ladies in town -Daddy would drop me off in the morning and pick me up at night when he went back home from working or drinking in town. The two ladies I usually worked for were very nice to me and treated me well. Both of them made me wash up real good when I got to their house to work, like the water out at the camp was not clean enough. I would have to stand out on the back porch with a bucket of water and make sure I was clean enough to go in their house. I think it was more their husbands' idea than the ladies.'

One of the ladies was Mrs. Shiloh - she was married to some kind of business big-shot at the bank. She had it pretty good, especially for those days. I would work hard for her and always did what she asked. She would always give me something to eat when I was done for the day while I waited for Daddy. I have no idea what I was being paid, because I never saw the money – Mrs. Shiloh always paid it directly to Daddy. I didn't ask about the money for fear I would get in bad trouble for 'being nosy' and get another beating.

Mrs. Shiloh was well spoken and I could tell she was very smart, just by the way she talked. I think she had gone to college. If she did work I didn't know about it, she was at home every day when I worked there. Mrs. Shiloh told some of her friends about how hard I worked and that I would do whatever they needed done. I helped several of them do jobs at their house off and on, usually the hard cleaning and floor scrubbing that had not been done for awhile.

I was grateful for the work, and Daddy liked that I made the needed cash for rent. On more than one occasion, Daddy dropped me off at someone's house and failed to pick me up in the evening; he more than likely got drunk and forgot where I was, so I spent the night in a couple of sheds nearby - and a barn once. It was too far to walk home and I was not the kind of girl that would hitch a ride from some stranger. That is just the way it was and I accepted that from Daddy. I didn't like it a bit but I had to do it, or else. I won't go into a lot of detail about what drinking does to a broken man when he is already down and does not seem to have any other options. I will just tell you that you never ever, ever, challenge a drunk - especially in those days when it was acceptable to beat your wife and kids.

Call the police, and they'd never show up; there were no agencies to call for help and no place to go to get away from the violence. We were poor farm workers that nobody cared if you got the crap kicked out of you by a man - you must have had it coming! Things were different back then - you did what you were told or got out on your own to find your own man who, by the way, could do the same thing to you with no laws to protect you.

I was a Fruit Tramp with no place to turn for help, that was the lot for young girls, and probably most wives back then, whether you were poor or not. You might think,'I would never have put up with that, I would have set out on my own and made my own way before I'd have put up with being beaten.' Well, it wasn't that easy - there was no place to go and no money to get there. You can't say you would have done anything different then we did, because societal mentality was so different before women's lib hit the fan in the '60s.

It is people of my era who fought hard to make sure future generations of women didn't have to suffer what we did as mere children. We paid the price with that kind abuse and made sure it ended with us.

One of the benefits of living at the Government Camp was that they had dances, and local musicians would perform once a month in a big grassy area on the edge of the property. We didn't have television - the radio is where we gathered to listen to the news of the day and some of the daily soap operas, variety shows and comedies for our entertainment. The radio was what most folks could afford and is all we ever had.

Dances were the big deal when I was a kid. Some of the local musicians would come out and put on a dance for the folks who lived in the camp and surrounding communities. Hundreds of people attended these hoedowns. It was a much anticipated social event in the local area, and many people traveled quite a way to come to the dances.

The music was made for dancing. So many of the men learned to dance while away in the service, that it became a reunion of sorts for many of them. Many of the men at the camp had friends from the service come to the dances. They would show off their dance moves and whoop it up for hours.

It was a party for the kids too. I enjoyed the music and watching everyone dance. Some were very good dancers and put on quite a show, flipping each other over their shoulder and under their legs, whew! I was impressed with the abilities of some of the couples. As I watched, I wondered if I would ever be that good or have someone to dance with like that.

Daddy was not much of a dancer, so him and Momma would just sit and watch all the action. Daddy would sneak liquor, as did many other men. I hated what liquor was doing to my Daddy; I could see the change in him and Momma. I think Momma was doing some drinking too, us kids would just stay out all night if both our parents were hitting the 'shine – it was better to avoid any problems.

We had a good friend in that camp and everybody just called him, Shooter. He was about my age and was the only kid in his family, so he was a little spoiled. Shooter's family had the cabin right behind ours. Because of the very thin walls, anytime we were at his cabin we could hear everything that was going on in our cabin with Momma and Daddy When both of them were 'shined up, it was really bad. The dances were just an excuse for them to drink and fight. Momma was always the loser and would have a black eye or busted lip the next day. Both of them were famous for saying, "Shut up, or I will slap the piss outta you."We all got sick of hearing that. What it really meant was that you better just do whatever it was and never say anything about it later, or take a beating for it if you did.

Some of the men Daddy was drinking with at the dances were the same ones he talked about hating because of their allotments of money from the Government, he was denied. I guess free liquor helps you change your opinion about people, because he would sit next to them all night like they were best old friends.

There was a big dance coming up for Christmas and we youngsters were looking forward to it. All us kids had been planning to try and dance this time, and we would practice out between the rows of cabins. Shooter would turn on his folk's radio and everyone would gather outside on the grass and act like a bunch of crazies trying to do some of the moves we had seen done by the adults. Of course, the moves never worked but, it didn't seem to matter; we were all having fun.

Many of the folks at the camp were talking about doing the Christmas dance somewhere other than the Government camp, so they could drink. We were pretty happy it still might happen though, no matter if there was drinking or not. After all, we had been practicing and were going to dance this time. I wanted the dance to happen and was hoping Shooter would dance with me. Christmas had been pretty much ignored by my family, and now finally at the age of 15, I wanted to have some fun with the holiday and celebrate. As usual, we didn't have a Christmas tree, and I had no doubt, there would be no gifts from Momma or Daddy— why break with tradition.

The dance would be my Christmas gift, and I was excited at the prospect of dancing with Shooter.

As luck would have it, the government cancelled the dance. The poster said they were sorry to announce that they couldn't obtain permission from the local officials to hold the Christmas Dance. We all knew it was because of all the talk from the returning service men about drinking. They seemed to think that because they fought in the war, rules no longer applied to them. We would hear them say, "I fought for this country and nobody's going to tell me I can't celebrate Christmas with a drink. They don't understand what I went through, and nobody tells me what to do anymore."

I respected the men who had to fight for our country, but this was no more than a bunch of drunks who wanted an excuse to drink and a place to do it.

I was afraid of what might become of the dance if it was moved to some farmer's barn. Anyone would be welcome and drinking would not be regulated. This would turn into a bad situation, and all of us kids knew it. We had seen and experienced first-hand how Momma and Daddy acted when they were full of 'shine.

Daddy started making friends quickly to see if there was any chance of finding a place to hold the dance. He asked everybody that would listen, telling them he had a band and plenty of returning servicemen to help put it on. I had never seen Daddy work so hard for a party. I was kind of impressed, but I'm sure it was more about the chance for drinking free 'shine than anything else.

Well, somehow Daddy pulled it off. He got the ranch foreman, where we had been working, to clean out an old tool shed at the back of the property for the big event. It was a long way back to where the old shed was but everybody in the camp helped kick in to get it cleaned up.

Several old pieces of broken down equipment had to be moved, and a couple men dug an outhouse while we worked on making a place to park cars in the tall grass along the water ditch.

After a couple hours, it was ready for the big event and all of us were happy for the work we had done. I did not like a couple of the men who were there because they already were drinking and popping off their mouths. They made a couple unseemly comments to me, too. If Daddy was to hear them, I knew he would punch them right in the mouth.

There were six of us kids there helping and those men had said things to all of us, even Shooter. I knew if Shooter's dad heard what they were saying, he would be in a fight too. I hated drunks and we wanted to stay away from all of them and have our own fun, without drinking.

Well, we did have the dance and it was the most fun I had in my life. I danced with Shooter a bunch of times and he was a pretty good dancer. We danced and talked all night. All of the kids were having a good time laughing, dancing and just listening to the music.

Some of the men who had been drinking pretty heavy were starting to make trouble; many people began leaving to avoid a fight. All of us kids stayed far away from that bunch but I watched to make sure nothing happened to our parents. Daddy was drinking with a couple of men, he was not making trouble and he too was staying away from the other drunks trying to start fights. I was proud of Daddy, because I had knew firsthand what 'shine did to him.

As the night went on, most of the trouble makers were made to go home, or they had passed out in their cars. All that was left were the ones who just wanted to celebrate Christmas and have a good time.

It started to get late and Momma wanted to leave. She asked me if I wanted to go. I told her I did because I could see she was tired and was kind of drunk. I asked Daddy if we could go and he told me to "walk" if I wanted to leave. He said he was staying. He was drunk and I knew if I pushed it, he would get mad and Momma would pay for it later. It was miles back to the cabin and it was late. It was getting cold and Momma and I were not about to walk. We were not in the mood to catch a ride with some drunk either, so we stayed.

Most of the revelers had left by this time, and Shooter also was leaving. It looked like I would be there alone with a bunch of drunks all talking loud and telling lies to each other.

After a short time, I had enough and headed for our car that was parked a short distance away. I took the blankets and made a pallet on the back floorboard, as I had so many times before in our travels. There was plenty of room for me to lie down and get some sleep while they drank the night away.

I have no idea how long I had been asleep when I could hear voices just outside the car. I didn't even bother to look as I recognized Daddy's loud drunken voice.

He was talking to the same man he had been drinking with all night. I could tell it was best for me to just stay quiet and keep the covers over my head. I drifted back to sleep, in spite of all the noise, and was comfortable with the warm blankets covering me. I hoped I would go unnoticed by them and could just sleep in peace.

The next thing I remember was someone opening the door to the back of the car where I was sleeping. I could hear the sound of another bottle of whiskey being opened, the tearing of the paper seal and the crack of the cork as it came out of the bottle. I wondered who it was,"Momma?,"I called out.

There was nothing but silence; I wondered if it was Daddy coming to hassle me in his drunkenness for his new drinking buddy's entertainment. I waited for a moment, and then all of a sudden someone was on top of me. The weight was overwhelming, and I was immediately terrified. Daddy would not do this, and I was sure it was not Momma as she would have said something to me. Again, nothing but silence. Then, someone was grabbing me all over!

A man started talking but I could not make out what was being said, I did not recognize the voice. I called out to Momma for help, again nothing but silence. I called out to Daddy and yelled at whoever was on top of me to, stop and get off of me. Still, silence.

I could smell his sour Whiskey breath from his heavy breathing but still not a word.

I started to fight to get him off of me but he was too strong and too heavy. I kept calling out to Momma and wondered why she could not hear me. They had just been outside the car door. I heard them talking there just moments ago. Didn't I?

Had I gone back to sleep and lost track of time? Had both of my parents gone back to the area where the dance had taken place and were too far away to hear my cries for help?

"Momma, Momma," I screamed as I struggled to fight off the attacker grabbing at my clothes and holding his hand over my face. He was pushing me down and kept putting his hand over my mouth so I couldn't cry out. He was so strong. I started to hit him hoping to get out from under him, but he was so heavy I was trapped and couldn't move under his weight. I was a prisoner in the back of that car, with no escape.

He was pulling at my dress and kept trying to kiss me, but I was able to push his face away from mine. His breath was strong with whiskey and so sour it made my stomach turn. He finally spoke and said, "Stop fighting and enjoy yourself." He said this over and over again. I was so scared. What was I supposed to be enjoying? He was hurting me. I started telling myself that this was not happening to me. I'm not really here; I must be having a nightmare. Wake up Betty Girl! Wake up!

What had started as the most fun I had in my life was now becoming the worst nightmare of my life. Why me I asked myself, why me?

Unable to fight him off I had to endure the greatest pain I had ever felt in my life. He was choking me and kept pushing my face into the floor. I could taste blood in my mouth. He repeatedly hit me in the head and face with his fist while yelling how good I looked and how much he had to pay for me. He said, "You cost me a whole bottle of good 'shine, you little bitch; now you're mine. Stop fighting and enjoy it."

I dared to look and see who was doing this to me. It was the man Daddy had been drinking with all night. Who was he and where was my Daddy - he wouldn't let this happen to me. I hurt so bad, I was losing more than he would ever know!

I kept asking myself how this man could be so strong and why he would do this to a little girl. I kept thinking I am going to die. There was another blow to my face, then another and another. I began to hyperventilate. Then things became fuzzy - I blacked out.

I don't know how long I was unconscious, but I slowly began to wake up. I was so confused. I did not know where I was. I could hear something, but I could not make out what it was; I could feel shaking, but I could not tell what was causing it. I was still crying out for help but could not hear my own cries - just ringing in my ears.

Have I died? Has my torture ended? I did not want to accept my fate. Death would be better than this. I couldn't hear. I couldn't see. I couldn't feel. Death had already taken me. I could not see the hand that had covered my face; I could not smell the stench of whiskey, only blood and I could only feel my body shaking with fear. I was so disconnected from my body - my life.

Why could no one hear my cries for help? Why did no one come to help to save me from death? I then begged for death to take me, "Please take me quickly, for I do not deserve this."

As quickly as it had begun, it was over. No more shaking. No more noise. The smell of whiskey still hung in the air, and I still could taste blood in my mouth.

Pain spread over my body. I could feel every blow I had taken. My face felt as if it would explode. My body still shaking and trembling, it was impossible for me to even sit up on the floor of the car. I wanted to move, but the pain was too great. I lay still, covered by my old blanket, a mouth full of blood. My dress was now tattered and torn to shreds. I was still trying to figure out what had just happened, I was so confused.

I was taken over by all the questions that needed to be answered, right now. Why me? What had I done to deserve this? What will happen now?

Immediately I blamed myself. It must have been my fault. I must have done something to make him do this to me! Does this happen to a lot of little girls, I asked myself? Laying there I felt that no one cared. No one helped me when I cried out. I did not matter. It was such a lonely feeling. Too scared to move and not wanting anyone to see me, I simply covered myself up and lay there, alone, waiting for answers and begging for the pain to stop.

I laid there for what seemed like an eternity in silence, questioning myself and finding only personal fault. All of a sudden the front doors came open; I could hear Momma and Daddy as they got in the car. I waited for something; I don't know what I was waiting for them to say, I just wanted someone to speak. There was nothing but silence from them. All I could hear was the sound of a whiskey bottle being opened as the cork was pulled out of it, and then the popping sound as it made its way out completely.

I tried to talk, but felt such pain in my face and jaw that I could barley move my mouth. Now I could feel the swelling all over my face as I ran my hands up and down my face and neck wiping the blood away and out of my eyes with what was left of my dress so I could see. My eyes were so swollen that it was impossible to open them. The ringing in my ears was so loud that I don't think I could have heard anyone, even if they did say something to me.

My hands were shaking so bad that I was hitting myself as I tried to wipe away the remaining blood from my face. I had a mouth full of blood and just let it run out of my mouth and onto my blanket so I would not get in trouble from Daddy for getting it in his car. I hurt so badly that I couldn't even cry, crying would have been too painful and I was still trying to understand what had happened. I was not sure what to cry about first.

I had to break the silence, "Momma." There was no response. I again said, "Momma."She promptly yelled in a drunker slur, "Shut up, or I will slap the piss out of you."

I could not believe what I was hearing. Did Momma and Daddy really sell me to that man? Did they know what he did to me?

I could hear both of them drinking from the jug of whiskey and could hear Daddy rattling some change in his change purse. I think it was to notify me of the price of whiskey.

So that's it, I asked myself? My life. My childhood. My innocence. Sold for a bottle of whiskey and a handful of change?

Momma and Daddy sold me for a bottle of whiskey?

"No, no," I kept repeating to myself, this didn't really happen - it became a mantra I repeated over and over on that long drive home.

How could I live with myself? What would others think about me? Would Shooter still like me? Am I am damaged goods, trash? Does Daddy think I am a tramp just like my sisters, now?

So many questions!

I no longer could trust Momma and Daddy to keep me safe from harm. I couldn't trust anyone. All of that was gone. I now knew I only could trust myself.

I was numb to the world, with the exception of one overriding feeling that I had never before experienced and had no idea how to control – hate. For the first time in my life, I knew true hate. It took over my mind. Every thought was filled with hate and everything had to pass through my hate as I tried to answer all the unanswered questions.

I now had no value. No one cared about me. I was trash and everybody knows what I did. It was my fault. I should have fought harder or screamed louder. I should have known better then to stay there. I had a chance to walk home but didn't. It is my fault!

The only emotion I had left was hate. My mind started to plan how to end it for everyone who did this to me. Why not? I had nothing to live for; shame, emotional pain, physical pain, the loss of trust – hate was all I had left. I felt so dirty and disgusting, I couldn't even stand myself. I was a tramp now!

How can I live again and face people with this hate and disconnect in my mind and my heart? Everybody will look at me and question my worth. Men will think I am easy and cheap. I knew I was all alone now. I realized I never really had the support from my family that I thought existed. It was all in my imagination and no one ever cared for me, they just used me for making money.

I was all alone.

Momma and Daddy left me in the car all night by myself. Both of them went into the cabin and I listened for a short time - they were fighting and Daddy was beating up Momma. The fighting and screaming, the sounds of Daddy hitting Momma was so loud it made me start shaking again; it was the sound of that filthy man hitting me. At some point I must have passed out from exhaustion.

In the morning, I awoke with so much pain I did not want to move, I was afraid it would kill me to move. Everything hurt, even inside me hurt. I still was bleeding and dried blood in my eyes made it hard to see.

I somehow managed to move from the back of the car. Getting out and standing there next to the open door, I looked back at the place where I had been lying, bleeding and crying all night. Seeing what was on the blankets made it clear that I had been raped and beaten. My clothes were torn and bloody, my face and body swollen from the attack. My heart and soul were broken and no longer had any value.

I was raped, I was raped, I was raped.

There, I said it, "I was raped."That was the ugly truth I had to face. I looked in the back of the car wondering why it happened, and I what it looked like - the place where my life changed.

I couldn't help but think Daddy would be so mad if I got blood in his nice car. I had to get to cleaning immediately. I looked at the blankets and wondered how I would get all the blood washed out before Momma saw them and scolded me for ruining her good blankets. I was distracting myself, I was afraid to look at myself in the mirror on Daddy's car. I hoped I would not see myself as I stood next to the car mirror, I was afraid to look straight into the mirror. I did not want to see the person I was, now.

How would I introduce myself to people from now on? "Hi, my name is Betty Jean, I was raped at 15 by a drunk my parents sold me to for a bottle of whiskey and a handful of change."

Momma and Daddy were supposed to protect me from such things.

My mind would not let me alone, I had to look, I had to see the new me. I struggled as I moved around the mirror. I finely got the courage to look; I was bloody, bruised and swollen, just like I expected. Surprisingly the physical marks were easy to look at. I was almost happy to see them. Those marks were proof that I did fight to protect myself. I tried to stop it. Thank you God for letting me see I am a fighter.

"Yes, I said to myself;" I did fight! I am not trash and no one owns me.

As quickly as I won that small victory, I again was overwhelmed with the hate I felt. I again could feel the punches, the choking, that smell. I felt hate for what he did and hate for all who let it happen.

I lose again. I am again his victim.

I had never known such hate. I never before had considered hate an acceptable feeling - so this was strange territory for me – in my new world; hate was not only okay, but necessary. It became my refuge.

I would need something to project this rage and anger onto so I did not have to bare all of the weight of this rape alone. Hate became my whipping boy of blame and a place for me to go when I needed to exercise my overwhelming emotion.

I was an easy target for my own hate, and I was always available for punishment.

I found my way into the cabin sometime late in the day, when I expected everybody to be out working in the fields. I sneaked in and washed up alone -wiping away all the blood from my face and hair.

I knew the bruises would heal, the swelling would go down and my body would no longer hurt. I suffered most from fear that my mind and soul would never heal. I questioned what would become of me?

I cried for yesterday, a day when I was so excited about life and my place in it. I wanted to take last night back. The music, dancing with Shooter, the fun and innocence of my childhood was no more than a fond memory now.

I prayed for tomorrow to come quickly. Maybe I will awaken from this bad dream and none of this will be true; that day never came. It was true, and I would never awaken the same person I was before that night.

The bruises were easy to see, so I stayed in the cabin until they were gone. Momma and Daddy told everybody in the camp I had measles and would infect them and their family if they came around.

As you might imagine, people stayed away. Measles killed a lot people back in those days because a vaccine was nonexistent.

I didn't look at Momma and Daddy for the next several months; we lived and worked together just like we had before that night, as if nothing ever happened. I wouldn't mention it to them the rest of my life and no explanation would ever be given.

Shooter and his family moved on to the next field and we, too, moved on to the next town. The next was just like the last. I never saw Shooter again, but I always hoped I would. I watched out the window as we traveled and looked as we came and left every camp, hoping to catch a glimpse of him. It was just a memory now.

Every town after the rape was just like the last, with the exception of one town, a town that will forever be different then all the rest. The town, where I would start to take control of my own life.

The rape and days to follow were like so many other things in my childhood - a time when I didn't feel I had a voice. I had been using denial and hate as the same word, the same thought.

I wanted to trust again, I talked and acted like I trusted others but, I didn't; I never really allowed myself to trust after the rape, and I became cynical.

It took me years to accept myself again and to believe I had value, value I deserved. I realized the shame was not mine to carry. The hate was only destroying me. I was suffering at my own hands.

I eventually gave all of it to the Lord; I set it at his feet and never looked back. It no longer was mine, and I would not allow anyone to victimize me again.

I will not be brushed off, pushed aside, or shoved down by anyone, ever!

My value is not decided by others, and if it is, it is not for my benefit I assure you. How people value me is done for their own benefit. I will not allow someone else to determine my life or value for me. I am strong, valuable and I matter. Call me whatever you want, but never again will I allow others to treat me poorly. Each generation after me will be better than the last, and I am willing to die trying to make that happen.

You can come along with me, or get out of my way. I will wait for no one.

Sin and hate have chased me all of my life. It has challenged me to fail every step of the way. I will not be defeated by the world.

I trust in God.
I forgive.
I love.
Faith and trust in God have championed all challengers.
I am Betty Jean, and I matter.

CHAPTER TWELVE

I Started Dreaming

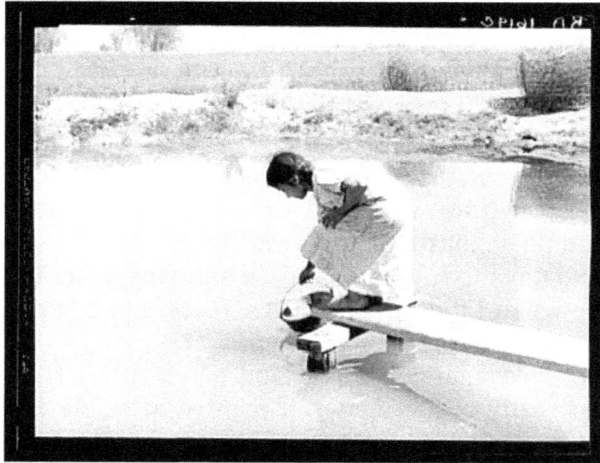

Shortly after the rape, I started dreaming of having my own life, one that did not allow other people to make decisions for me.

I was 15 years old, but had lived enough life to make decisions about what was not ever going to happen to me again. The only way to make sure I was not victimized again was to begin planning my own future.

It took some time for me to recover from the rape, but it was even harder to recover from what Momma and Daddy allowed to happen. Distrust was now a constant in my life. I never felt completely safe with my parents from that point on. My life had changed. I understood and accepted responsibility for my own well being and place in life.

I started dreaming about how things would be different for me and for my future family someday.

As the music and fond memories of the dance played over and over in my head, I started to plan how my leaving the family would be different than that of my two older sisters. I would not chase my imagination, as Daddy put it, I would make sure I used my imagination to fuel my dreams and make a plan.

I no longer would allow Daddy to make me work for nothing. When we went to a field, I would sign my own work permit and tell them the money I earned was mine and it had to be given to me. It sometimes was impossible to get my money because Daddy would tell the cashiers to give my pay to him, and he told them he would make sure I got it. He never gave me any of my money that he collected. It only happened a few times before I wised up and made sure to be there to pick up my own pay.

Needless to say, it was a little more than strained in my family. I would give them some of my pay to cover my costs, but the days of not getting even one penny of my money were over.

I saved and planned for three more years and lived with my parents until I felt I had what I needed to make my own way. Keeping my own earnings and keeping it hidden away from Daddy was difficult. Daddy would try to guilt me out of some of it nearly every day. I knew he wanted it for 'shine even though he would say it was for food for the other kids.

I would not give my dream away, not to Daddy or anybody.

I had been dreaming about living in California, maybe in Hughson, because I always felt welcome there. Welcome and accepted is what I wanted for my future family. I wanted for them what I never had as a child; to be a real part of a community and not have to live on the fringes of society.

All those years of working for nothing, being beaten for saying the wrong thing, and told I had to work instead of going to school, had come to an end.

I went to the local libraries as much as I could and taught myself to read, how to calculate basic math and to understand the fundamentals of science. I still wanted to try and graduate from high school someday.

We still moved so often that it was unlikely I would ever achieve that dream, as long as I still lived with my parents. It almost was like they kept us on the move so I could not make my way to my own life.

Still, I worked and saved every penny I earned until I had a chance to leave and make my dreams start to come true. The first dream was to be on my own and be able to decide for myself what I wanted to do from day to day. For me, there would be no more dances or parties. All of my energy would be to serve my dream.

What Daddy said about the other girls chasing their imagination and not their dreams played out in my mind over the last few years. I wouldn't let myself fail and be subject to what had become of my older sisters. We would see them on occasion as we traveled some of the same roads and ended up working in some of the same fields.

If we did end up working in the same field, my sisters would move on before Daddy found out what was going on with them. Every time I saw my sisters they were beaten up or beaten down. I knew I would never be beaten again, and it only strengthened my resolve to succeed.

My sisters had no plan except leaving home. Maybe Daddy was right about why they left. He seemed to know what was in store for their future. Chasing their imagination provided nothing for them and seemed to be stealing away their hope, too. It was very hard for me to see them treated and down trodden; I could do nothing for them. I promised myself it would be different for me.

Midge and Donnie eventually came back and stayed with us from time to time -sometimes to heal up from an abusive husband, or moved back with the family because they were pregnant. Both sisters expected us to provide for them and openly refused to work in the fields. I loved them, but I would not abandon my dreams because of their failure. I had worked very hard for so long and I no longer could bear to submit to this lifestyle.

The two of them moved in and out until I left at age 18 to be on my own. It was always the same when they came back. Resentments grew each time they returned, because we only worked for ourselves - not sharing as much as in the past. It stayed that way the rest of our lives.

My sisters and brother resented me for not giving into them every time they asked for money. It was as though they expected me to take care of them forever. I would have my own family to take care of and I was done taking care of them financially. My dreams did not include having all the life sucked out of me by lazy, demanding siblings.

Most of my dreams in those early years did not include any of my family - I blamed them for some of what had happened. Some of it was my fault for trusting my life to others; I was not going to trust my future and dreams to someone else ever again.

The rape was the single event that changed my life the most. I spent time thinking about it most every day, sometimes every moment. I had anger and trust issues. I was afraid of the dark. I always slept up against the door of the cabin on the floor to make sure no one was able to come in at night and hurt me.

I wouldn't talk to just anybody because I was afraid they wanted to lure me away and rape me. I was not a man hater, but I was making sure that I was in control if I talked to a man.

I stayed inside most of the time and always watched out when I would go somewhere like the library to make sure no one was following me. It was very hard for many years, and I had nobody in whom to confide. Momma and Daddy had sold me for a bottle of Whiskey and a handful of change, so I had nothing to say to them. I knew the police would do nothing and I would only face humiliation from them, so that wasn't even a consideration. There was no such thing as a Rape Crisis center, so I suffered with this on my own - I am sad to know many other women endured the same abuse.

Sometimes it was more then I could stand. It played over in my mind and I questioned why it happened to me, wondering why I could not fight him off, and more importantly, how parents could allow that to happen to their daughter.

At times, I wanted to be angry and thought about what I would do to my parents for selling me. I thought about hurting someone else just to try and get it out of my mind. I remembered all those preachers over the years talking about forgiveness for others and letting go of anger, but I was nowhere close to letting any of the anger go.

I felt myself slipping away from my dreams at times, and wondering if it was all just a lie - happiness and peace. I continued to turn to my old Bible for distraction, hope and answers - as I had nothing else that could take me away from where I was and who I was there with.

I wish I could remember where I was reading in my Bible that day, the day everything changed for me, just like the day I was raped. I was reading my Bible out on the front porch of the cabin we were living in, and all of a sudden it came to me how I was allowing myself to feel pity and continuing to allow myself to be a victim of the filthy beast who had raped me, and the so called parents who profited from it.

I knew at that very moment I had to make a choice to recover from it -to stop being a victim and start living my dreams - without allowing outside influences to lead me astray. All along I had allowed myself to be controlled by that day and that rape. Well, that was to be over now I told myself. I no longer would allow anybody to control me or what I did. I would make my own choices and decisions and would not worry that someone would control me or make decisions for me. No one would ever brush me off, push me aside or hold me down. I would not allow a man to control me in any way, and would do what I had to so my children never have to live this way.

I would fight, at anybody's expense, to protect my own from those conditions. I would teach my children to be fighters and keep them from being controlled by others, as I had been for all of my childhood. I would teach them to never start a fight but be able to finish it with pride and respect. My children would be kind and loving and they would be a part of a community where they could be safe to grow and learn.

My children would be able to have food on the table every night and not have to scavenge from garbage cans and beg, as I had too. They would have clean clothes and be able to go to school every day like, I wanted to. They wouldn't have to work in hot dirty fields while the other kids went to school. My children would graduate from high school with the same kids with whom they started kindergarten.

I would not be a victim any longer or ever again. I was finally free!

But, I quickly realized that nothing is free, especially freedom. I had to pay a heavy cost to live out my dreams the rest of my life.

I never found the perfect balance of fulfilling my dreams, protecting my kids and doing it in a way where everybody would be happy. It seemed as though somebody was always unhappy with me for being too protective and fighting for my family.

Everybody has their past and from those experiences, finds a way to make their future work. I was no different and didn't accept criticism from those who couldn't understand my childhood. It wasn't that I blamed them for my childhood, but unless a person lived like me, and thousands did, you wouldn't ever really understand from what I was protecting my children.

I am a survivor and have persevered in spite of my family. I have realized that the same thing that made me strong' early in my life (my family), was the same thing that was my greatest weakness' later in my life. It is for all of us to be cautious of our strengths so we do not allow them to become a weakness when we most need protection and support.

Epilog

Every generation has challenges and triumphs, mine was no different. I wanted to tell my story as an encouragement for children to start talking to their parents and grandparents about that time so long ago.

As strange as it sounds, I would not do it, (my childhood) any other way. It is my life and I take full responsibility for what I made of it.

I am happy to tell you that all of my children lived in the same house their entire childhood. They did go to high school with the same kids with whom they started kindergarten, and I think they are still friends with many of them today.

I lost track of the kids I went to school with, so I love to hear the stories my kids tell me about their childhood friends and what they are doing today.

My kids have all done well in their own right and have been successful in many ways.

A couple of them went to college and one of them graduated from a very prestigious University. He has traveled all over the world with his business and brings me gifts and stories about where he has been. I always wanted to travel like that, and see the world; now I get to through his eyes.

My children married good people and I have enjoyed watching them grow, raise families and help them avoid what was so costly for me in my life; I guess that's what we do as parents and grandparents.

I love my family and my grandkids and even great grandkids. I have lived a full life and my dream of making a better life for my kids has come true.

I took Little Granny's suggestion to dream. I followed Daddy's advice to not just chase my imagination. I planned my dreams, and then set out to work for it. It really works. All the hard work was worth it. I would do it all over again for my family.

I have been blessed and my dreams have been fulfilled.

I freely pass life experiences on to my family and ask that everybody who reads my story do the same for their family. I know of no greater gift then making sure my family knows from where they came, and of those who made a way for them.

I can now begin to rest, as my children carry on the family knowledge, and name for future generations.

I am almost 80 years old, now, and have lived a full and complete life.

It was very hard for me, but I forgave Momma and moved back to Arkansas to help take care of her in her last years. Momma had been sick and had Alzheimer's the last five years of her life. I would go visit her every week and take some things to her hoping she would remember me. Every week I would arrive and go to her room wondering if today would be the day she would look at me and call me by my name; every week it was the same blank stare - each time my heart would cry.

I would sit and hold Momma's hand and tell her stories about things I remembered as a child while she stared out the window. It was difficult, but it seemed to do me some good after I recovered from the initial hurt.

I hated what Alzheimer's had done to Momma - it had taken her away from me and left a shell of the person Momma once was. I did find some comfort in holding her hand and just resting for a time - after all those years of constantly being on the go from one town to the next. Momma was accepted by all the staff at the facility she was living in, and for that I was happy.

Momma did not have many possessions. Daddy kept a few things at the cabin where they were living in Gentry, Arkansas. He thought she would come home someday, even though she did not remember him when we visited her at the Care Center. I would sit on one side of the bed holding her hand and Daddy on the other doing the same. We would sit for hours, sometimes never saying a word; we were lost in our own thoughts and memories. Sometimes, Daddy would tell me what he was thinking about as I drove him back to his little cabin; it was comforting to know he really loved Momma all those years.

Momma passed away in 1990 and was buried in a cemetery in Arkansas; she enjoyed living her last years in that part of the country. After Momma passed, Daddy kind of quit. He had other family but he felt very alone without Momma. I would visit every week at the cabin and he always left the closet door open so he could see Momma's clothes hanging in there. I think he wondered why Momma never came back home, and couldn't find a way to live without her.

The cabin was much like the ones we had lived in most of my childhood - small one-room cabins with no running water and only one light in the ceiling. The bed was the biggest piece of furniture in the place and they had one big sitting chair, besides the two chairs at the small kitchen table where I remember them sitting when I visited many times. Momma and Daddy sitting and sipping coffee, Daddy called it cowboy coffee because of the way Momma would make it -boil water with coffee grounds in it, and when the coffee was good and burnt, it was ready to drink. I could not stand it, but Momma and Daddy had gotten used to it over all those years of not having any other way of brewing coffee.

I would do a little cleaning at the cabin when I visited just to help out Momma and give her a break. It was real easy to clean, I would grab a small bucket of water from the little creek next to the cabin and wipe the small kitchen counter before moving on to the five minutes of dusting what few things they had.

Momma did not like me fussin' over things so she would tell me not to do it because she already had cleaned. I think I did the cleaning more for me than anything else.

One small table with two chairs, one bed and one big overstuffed chair next to a small crate on which Daddy used to set his tobacco can - that was all that was in the cabin.

Momma always sat at the little kitchen table and Daddy sat in that big old chair, he only weighed about 100 pounds by this time, and that chair would gobble him up and make him look so small. As a kid my dad looked so big to me, and now he looked so small in that big chair.

Daddy got sick not long after we buried Momma. I think he wanted to be with her again and if it was not to be here on earth then he would meet her in heaven.

I would go to the hospital every day and see him so we could talk and laugh. Daddy was so sick and I had a hard time watching as he kind of gave up on life missing Momma so bad. He would tell me how he missed her and asked why he had to be alone without her. I had no answer and would just hold his hand and listen.

Daddy had been in the hospital for several weeks and only seemed to get worse each day. The nurses told me he would not eat and would only take his medication if he was made to, and that would come after he called them some less then flowery names. The hospital called one morning and told me to come right down, Daddy was demanding I come get him.

I went there and when I walked in the room Daddy was sitting up in his bed and had a glow about him I had not seen for a long time. I was so excited to see him like that, I could not contain myself. Tears were running down my face and he was smiling the whole time I was there that day. We had a great day talking. He told me he wanted to go home - he asked me to take him back to his cabin because he wanted to be home with his own stuff around him, not in some hospital where he had nothing of his own.

I told him I would get the cabin ready and take him home the next day. When I started to leave, he pointed to a paper bag on the floor next to the door and told me to get some of his clothes so he could have his own things to wear home. I grabbed the paper bag and off I went, I was so happy to see Daddy smile and laugh, I cried all the way home.

I went to the cabin and got Daddy's coveralls and boots so he would have them for the trip home from the hospital. The cabin looked so empty without him or Momma there, but I was happy Daddy would be returning soon. We would sit and talk again while we listened to the small creek running alongside the cabin – the water's gentle tumble over polished stones was comforting.

When I got to the hospital the next morning the door to Daddy's room was closed. I went inside and the doctor was there beside Daddy's bed. As soon as I looked at the doctor I knew something was wrong, it was my worst nightmare, Daddy was very sick and they did not expect him to make it through the day.

I prayed with Daddy for awhile and held his hand as I talked to him and told him I forgave him for everything that had happened. I told him I loved him and how I would miss him when he was gone. I told him to tell Momma I loved her too because Alzheimer had stolen her away before I had a chance to tell her myself.

I asked one of the nurses to help me dress him in his coveralls so he could go home in his own clothes just like he asked.

Daddy went home that day, he passed quietly in the afternoon as I sat and held his hand. I was devastated and felt so alone when he was gone, I was alone and scared of not having my parents with me any longer.

I waited several days before I went to the cabin again. The last time I was there I was so excited because Daddy was coming home and we would spend time together again. I guess I was thinking Daddy would be coming home to his home here on earth, I then knew, he was talking about going to his eternal home in Heaven.

When I got to the door I paused before I went in inside to make sure I was ready - ready for it to be empty, truly empty.

I was not prepared for what happened when I walked in, I was not alone at all, I could feel Momma and Daddy there, and almost was as if I could hear them talking.

There was Momma sitting at that small kitchen table sipping coffee and Daddy sitting in his big chair looking out the big window down to the creek. I could hear the water running slowly by just as it had years unnumbered. The smell of strong coffee hung in the air and the smoke from Daddy's cigarette moved slowly around in the room, just as I would always remember.

The door to the closet was left open and I could see Mommas dresses hanging there, waiting for her to decide for the day which of the three it would be. I stood and waited to see if it was true, I wanted it to be true and to wake up from a bad dream. I waited for Daddy to say, "Come on in, Betty Girl, have a seat and rest for awhile."

I waited, but it was only silence.

I knew I had to accept what had come of them, I felt so alone at that moment, like never before. I looked around the room and took stock of two lives that had meant so much to me - not perfect lives, but ones I loved and cared for, ones I had forgiven long ago.

I sat in Daddy's chair, as I sank down in it I felt as though he was wrapping his arms around me, giving me the comfort I so desperately needed at that moment. I felt as though he wanted me to know he was looking out for me.

As I looked past Momma's dresses hanging there, starring out that big window down at the creek, just like Daddy did, I wondered how I would remember them - how I would know they really loved me, too.

As I sat there quietly and looked around the room for the last time I knew things would never be the same, my life would be different from now on. I cried for the love I knew I would miss, even if it was not spoken I knew I was loved.

I looked at all of the things that remained of their lives - what would I keep to remind me of my Momma and Daddy. Can anything keep alive for me the feelings we once felt, the day Daddy lifted me on to his shoulders, is it possible to feel like that ever again?

I walked over to the open closet and took Momma's dresses in my hands, I moved them up to my nose and I could smell Momma, she loved me and I loved her. They felt soft against my face and they seemed to comfort me like she had done so many times before. I miss Momma!

I placed them in a box to take home, I would decide later what to do with them.

As I looked at Daddy's coveralls folded neatly on the small shelf I wondered if he knew how much I loved him, I smelled them too because I wanted to feel close to him one last time. I added the coveralls to the dresses in the box - they were pretty worn and would have little value or use to anyone else - to me they were priceless remembrances, it was all I had left. The shoes and other things in that small closet fit into the one small box.

As I closed the door I discovered and old cigar box on the floor behind the door. I put it in the grocery box with all the other things and cleaned out the remaining things into a couple other boxes to take home.

It was going to be hard to leave behind this place - a place where so many wrongs of my childhood seemed to melt away - where I had learned to forgive and accept my childhood. I no longer wanted to blame them and I did not want to be angry for the rest of my life, because I knew a day would come when I no longer could tell them they were forgiven by me. I kept saying out loud how much I loved them - like they were there in the room with me. In my mind, they were there. I wanted to leave but could not, not yet. I sat back in Daddy's chair and pulled some things out of the box and into my lap, hanging on for just a few more moments, it was hard to let go.

Looking back into the box I wondered what the small cigar box from behind the door was, and why it was behind the door where nobody could see it. I picked it up and could hear some things rattling around inside. I paused because I was afraid I would discover something bad, something Daddy did not want anybody to see."Please Lord, protect my heart and keep me away from judgment in all matters of my Momma and Daddy," I kept repeating to myself.

I looked at the box without opening it for a few minutes and tried to remember why it looked so familiar to me. I know I had seen it before, but could not remember where. It was just an old cigar box and looked like it was a hundred years old with all the paint worn off and the corners rounded and torn.

The lid was real loose and I had to be very careful as I opened it, it was falling apart. As I looked inside I was relieved to see some old papers, a tobacco pipe and some loose change; a couple pennies.

I laughed at myself now having worried about what I would find.

I shuffled some of the papers around and started to take them out one-by-one and look at them.

An old paper with a few addresses and names of Daddy's relatives, a car title to the blue Plymouth Daddy got for us in Hughson from "old Creekmore" the horse trader, and a couple pennies that were all worn out and discolored was all that was inside the box.

Why would Daddy keep such things, I wondered. I guess they were important events in his life and he carried them around for all those years to remind him of where he had been. Then, I discovered an envelope stuck in the bottom of the box. It almost was too big to fit inside that small box and Daddy had just forced it in all the way to the bottom. The envelope was all yellow from all the years it must have been in the bottom of that box.

As I looked I could see some faded writing on the face of the envelop, it read,"Betty Girl," written in pencil in Daddy's handwriting. I found a piece of folded brown paper inside and I pulled it out. I began looking out the window and again asking God to prepare my heart for what I would find.

As I unfolded the brown paper I remembered where I had seen that old cigar box before. It was all those years and miles ago when I was a little girl, the day I first went to school. Out in front of the school that day when I was so excited to go to school with my beautiful new dress and shoes.

Daddy had taken a penny out of that cigar box and gave to me to keep me safe, to give me luck. The old box he pulled out from under the seat of the truck, his "box of secrets."

I looked back in the box and stared at the pennies inside, was one of those pennies the one Daddy had given me to keep in my shoe, It could be, I bet it was, I wanted it to be as I took them out and held them in my hand. I held them tight and told Daddy how much that meant to me those days when I watched men getting on that bus to go to war, and how I believed in what he had told me about the penny because he never had to leave.

I remembered that little boy and my teacher Mrs. Brenda who cried when they saw their loved one get on that bus, maybe seeing him for the last time.

I knew my Daddy loved me; he kept that penny all those years so he could remember that day too, the day he lifted me up on his shoulders and showed me how much he loved me. Tears started to run down my face as I thought about that day and what it meant to me, and now I knew it meant as much to Daddy.

I wondered how he had managed to keep that for so long as much as we moved and, how he had kept it hidden away.

My hands were shaking, I could hear paper rattling and it reminded me about the piece of brown paper I was holding in my hand from inside the envelop.

It was time; I had to look at the folded paper to see what Daddy had kept with my name on it for all those years in his, box of secrets.

As I unfolded it, a rush of emotion came over me, tears running down my face and onto the box- I remembered what I had made that first day of school so long ago, I was holding it in my hands again after more than 60 years.

It was the little handprint of colored paint, the one I was so proud of that first day of school. I remembered how I felt when I gave it to Daddy.

As if it was just yesterday, I could see and hear myself telling Daddy I made him something and then watching as he looked. I remember his smile and can still hear the paint cracking as he folded it and put it in the front pocket of his overalls.

At the time I guess I did not completely understand what I had made for Daddy and had no idea he would keep it for the rest of his life - but he had kept it, and seeing it again was more then I could imagine.

I sat in Daddy's chair, and cried as I remembered all he meant to me. How I loved him. Forgotten were all the transgressions of my childhood, and all I once thought was so mean and hateful of my Daddy.

I felt so comfortable sitting there with his arms around me, protecting me from all that the world brings. I wondered how I could honor my Daddy's memories now that he was gone. Now that I knew how much he loved me, I wondered how things would be if I could turn back time and once again be Daddy's little Betty Girl.

I was sad to see the sunset on this time of my life and could not hold back the tears -I cried for my childhood. It was time to forgive; to let go of anything for which I blamed my Momma and Daddy. I spoke out loud as I uttered those words I had carried on my heart for all those years, but never found a way to say them to my parents when they were still here.

I again looked at that little handprint and wondered what Daddy thought of it, really thought of it, and why he never spoke of it the rest of his life.

I again held that envelop up looking inside it to see if I might find another reminder of my Daddy's love. Yes, something else is in there. Inside that envelop was another folded paper, one that had shared space with my little handprint. I guess he wanted to capture what that gift had meant to him so long ago because it was a note he had written and placed with the handprint.

On the paper was written:

1 CORINTHIANS 13:4-8

"Love is very patient and kind, never jealous or envious, never boastful or proud, never haughty or selfish or rude. Love does not demand its own way. It is not irritable or touchy. It does not hold grudges and will hardly even notice when others do it wrong.

It is never glad about injustice, but rejoices whenever truth wins out. If you love someone you will be loyal to him no matter what the cost. You will always believe in him, always expect the best of him, and always stand your ground defending him.

All the special gifts and powers from God will someday come to an end, but love goes on forever."

There was also another note, it read;

"Now," I want you to close your eyes, close your eyes and listen with your heart, open it to your own time so long ago.

Do you see it, do you?

Do you see that little hand all covered in paint as you press it on the paper?

Now lift up your hand, do you see what you have made, do you see your little print? That is you, that is your mark, it is like no other in the world.

Do you see how your fingers left a heavy impression out on t he end; now look back here where it is real light. Do you see all t he detail? It is all smeared and hard to see any detail out where the impression is heavy.

In life, it requires both a heavy touch and a light one for it to be complete, to create the whole picture; for one is incomplete without the other."

I think that was Daddy's way of telling me he loved me and, his apology for what had been my childhood.

As I look at that little handprint, I find the greatest detail in the light touch.

I spent much of my childhood and much of my life for that matter, only seeing the heavy touch, and believing that the heavy touch was the only one that existed. I missed so much of what life offered because of my narrow vision.

Little Granny tried to tell me, show me how to experience both sides of life and she always talked about taking time to experience the moment. Now I know what she was trying to say.

Maybe it is time we all look for the light touch in our lives for that is where the greatest detail of our lives will be found - that special moment in time when our heart is good with the world. It may be a moment created by a loved one or something you see or hear. God has given me the eyes and ears to experience and enjoy all he has created, it is my heart that must be willing to stop and "smell the roses."

I looked back through my childhood for the lightest touch from my Daddy; I found it in places I had never examined before. I now recognize the blessings and love my parents tried to express, I now believe in love.

Thank you Momma and Daddy, I love you!

"Betty Girl"

Betty Jean Taylor
Chowchilla, California
2012